GOD SPAKE BY MOSES

GOD SPAKE BY MOSES

Oswald T. Allis

B.D., Ph.D., D.D.

An Exposition of the Pentateuch.

PRESBYTERIAN AND REFORMED PUBLISHING CO.
PHILLIPSBURG, NEW JERSEY

THE PRESBYTERIAN AND REFORMED
PUBLISHING COMPANY

First published in 1951

ISBN: 0-87552-103-7

Library of Congress Card Catalogue Number: 58:59922

PREFACE

READERS of *The Life of Faith* will recognize in this volume the Lessons on the Pentateuch which appeared in its pages during the last quarter of 1949. They have been revised and considerably enlarged, but are in other respects substantially the same. The general principle which was followed in preparing them was that they should deal with the Bible itself, and with theories about the Bible only insofar as this was necessary to show their agreement or disagreement with its teachings. For while it is undoubtedly true that modern scientific research has thrown much welcome light upon the Bible, upon our knowledge of Bible lands and Bible times, it is nevertheless true that the Bible is its own best interpreter, and that the aim of the Bible student should always be to find out what the Bible actually teaches and not to try to impose upon it meanings which, however attractive and well-established they may seem to be, are clearly not the meanings which the Bible itself warrants and approves.

It is the hope of the writer that this little book will help its readers to appreciate more fully the wonderful self-evidencing unity and authority of the Bible. For this the Pentateuch is especially adapted. It lays the foundation of all that follows, both in the Old Testament and in the New. It points forward to the coming of One who would be like unto yet far greater than Moses, in whom as the promised Saviour God has made fully known His grace and truth for a sin-cursed world. God spake by Moses to His people of old; and those who will hearken to Moses today will find that he is pointing them to One who said of the great Lawgiver of ancient Israel, "He wrote of Me."

WAYNE, PA.   OSWALD T. ALLIS

PUBLISHER'S PREFACE

God Spake By Moses was first published in 1951 by Marshall, Morgan, and Scott, Ltd., of London. It was distributed in the United States under our imprint and in Canada by the Evangelical Publishers. Several British printings having been exhausted, we are reprinting it, slightly revised, in a paper-back edition.

God Spake By Moses is a brief popular exposition of the Pentateuch which assumes its Mosaic authorship. Much of its contents appeared originally in *The Life of Faith* (London). We agree with the *Southern Presbyterian Journal* that the "book is a 'must' for every minister and layman who would discover the real meaning and true interpretation of the first five books of the Bible."

Dr. Oswald T. Allis, one of the most prominent and erudite Old Testament scholars of our generation, holds to the biblical viewpoint that Moses wrote the first five books of the Bible and that the prophet Isaiah wrote the entire Book of Isaiah. He has answered the "higher critics" in two authoritative works, *The Five Books of Moses* and *The Unity of Isaiah*. Both titles are being widely used in conservative schools as texts and for collateral reading. Dr. Allis is also the author of *Revision or New Translation?*, *Revised Version or Revised Bible?*, and *Prophecy and The Church;* we plan to publish his *The Old Testament: Its Claims and Critics* early in 1959.

Dr. Allis holds academic degrees from the University of Pennsylvania, Princeton University, Princeton Theological Seminary, and the University of Berlin. For nineteen years he taught in the Department of Semitic Philology at Princeton Theological Seminary and for seven years was a professor in the Old Testament Department at Westminster Theological Seminary. Since 1929 he has been an associate editor of the *Evangelical Quarterly* (Edinburgh) and is currently a contributing editor of *Christianity Today*.

CHARLES H. CRAIG, *Editor*

CONTENTS

GENESIS

IN OUR English Bibles the Old Testament has four main divisions: the Law (Genesis–Deuteronomy), Historical books (Joshua–Esther), Poetical books (Job–Song of Solomon), Prophetical books (Isaiah–Malachi). Since the Law is composed of five books, Jewish scholars called it "the five-fifths of the Law", and Greek scholars called it the "Pentateuch"—the five books. Elsewhere in the Bible we find frequent references to "the law" or "the law of Moses". In some cases this may refer to the whole Pentateuch, in others to only part of it. The titles of these five books which appear in the Authorized Version and other versions, "The first book of Moses, commonly called Genesis", etc., are no part of the text. But they express the well-grounded belief of the Church, both Jewish and Christian, that the Pentateuch was written by Moses, "the man of God".

The Pentateuch covers the period of sacred history from the Creation to the death of Moses. It falls naturally into two parts. Genesis deals with the pre-Mosaic period to the death of Joseph. The other four books contain the history, laws, and institutions of the Mosaic age: Exodus describes the oppression, the deliverance, the journey to Sinai, the giving of the law, the erection of the tabernacle; Leviticus is a manual of laws given at Sinai for the priests who were to be the ministers of the tabernacle; Numbers covers the period from the dedication of the tabernacle at Sinai in the second year to the arrival at Jordan in the fortieth year; Deuteronomy consists largely of the farewell addresses of Moses delivered just before his death.

The Book of Genesis[1] is the longest of the "five books", and its fifty chapters divide readily into four nearly equal parts: the pre-patriarchal history (i. 1–xi. 32); Abraham (xii. 1–xxv.

[1] The title "Genesis" was taken over from the Greek (LXX) Version, which uses it to render the word "generation" (e.g. Gen. ii. 4). The Jews call the book "Bereshith" (in the beginning), using for a title its opening phrase.

7

11); Isaac and his sons (xxv. 12–xxxvi. 32); Joseph (xxxvii. 1–
l. 26). The death of Abraham (xxv. 8) divides Genesis into two
nearly equal parts. The history is told largely in terms of
biography. Three-quarters of the book are mainly concerned
with the lives of three men: Abraham, Jacob, and Joseph.

While the analysis just given indicates the general content
of Genesis, the book itself supplies us with a more detailed
analysis which is of great importance. It is indicated by eleven
titles or headings, in each of which the word "generations"
appears, and which divide the book into twelve sections of
very varying length. The "generations" are the following:

(1) The heavens and the earth (ii. 4)
(2) Adam (v. 1)
(3) Noah (vi. 9)
(4) The Sons of Noah: Shem, Ham and Japheth (x. 1)
(5) Shem (xi. 10)
(6) Terah (xi. 27)
(7) Ishmael, Abraham's son (xxv. 12)
(8) Isaac, Abraham's son (xxv. 19)
(9) Esau, who is Edom (xxxvi. 1), the father of the Edomites
     in Mount Seir (xxxvi. 9)[1]
(10) Jacob (xxxvii. 2)

In most cases, as the word "generations" implies, the heading
introduces a section which is concerned with the sons or descendants of the one named in it. For example, the section
entitled "the generations of Terah" relates the life of Abraham,
Terah's most famous son. The "generations of Jacob" begin
with the words "Joseph being seventeen years old". But "the
generations of Noah" deal largely with the Flood, in which
Noah played the conspicuous rôle, which shows that the word
"generations" is not to be taken too strictly, especially since the
life of Noah overlapped that of Shem by 450 of Shem's 600
years and included the Flood, its most important event.

[1] Since the headings in xxxvi. 1, 9 are exactly alike, it would be
natural to assert that these two Generations should be treated as No. 9
and No. 10 instead of being brought together under one head. But
while Esau's withdrawal to Seir was a matter of great importance, since
it left Canaan to the descendants of Jacob and postponed a conflict
which later became acute, this hardly seems to justify the exceptional
assigning of two independent and co-ordinate Generations to him.
Furthermore to treat these Generations as separate and distinct would
increase the total to eleven, while ten seems to be the number intended.

GENESIS i. 1–ii. 3, which tells of the creation of "the heaven and the earth", constitutes the basis or foundation of the series of "generations" that follow it. It is therefore of fundamental importance. It consists of a summary, an explanatory, and a detailed statement.

(i) *The Summary Statement:* "In the beginning God created the heaven and the earth." Every word is important. Here we have the starting-point (in the beginning), the ultimate Reality (God), and the phenomenal universe (heaven and earth) brought into being (created) by Him. These are the ultimates; and the Ultimate of ultimates is God. The word "God" (Elohim) occurs thirty-five times in the thirty-four verses of this section, almost always as subject. In this way the Supreme Being, who is before all things and who has made all things, is impressively introduced. This is the key-note of the Bible. The Bible is the Word of God, not only because God is its author, but because God and His doings are its pervasive theme. *Elohim* is a plural form; but throughout the Old Testament it is regularly construed as singular when used of the true God, which indicates that it is a plural of majesty or excellence, and has no connection with polytheistic notions.

"Create" (*bara*) is a rare word in the Old Testament, and it is always used of an act or activity of God. It does not necessarily mean creation *out of nothing* (*ex nihilo*); but this is clearly implied. "The heaven and the earth" cover what we call the universe, and are more fully explained by what follows. "In the beginning" has reference to the commencement of God's creative work as here briefly summarized.

(ii) *The Explanatory Statement* (verse 2). The connection between verses 1 and 2 has been much discussed. The most natural view is that verse 2 describes "the earth" proleptically as consisting of unorganized matter (chaos) before the acts of the six creative days transformed it into a beautifully ordered *cosmos.* Two other views must be mentioned: (*a*) that verse 1 should be rendered, "When God began to create the heaven and the earth, the earth was . . ." This is grammatically possible. But it is awkward and implies the pre-existence of matter, a dualistic notion utterly foreign to the Bible. (*b*) The catastrophe or interval theory, according to which verse 1 describes a primordial creation of wondrous beauty which was reduced to chaos (in connection with the fall of Satan?); so

understood the rest of the chapter describes the rehabilitation
of the earth to be the dwelling place of man. This interpretation gained favour about a century ago as a means of bringing
Genesis i into harmony with the findings of geologists. It was
claimed that verse 2 represents a vast timeless interval in which
the "geological ages" can be placed and regarded as preceding
a six-day re-creation of the present earth. It finds no clear
support elsewhere in Scripture, and is faced with serious difficulty in interpreting verses 14–19. See Appendix.

"Spirit" (of God) might also be rendered "wind" or "breath".
We cannot affirm that the doctrine of the personality of the
Holy Spirit is taught here. The meaning is not explained.
But it is to be noted that the "Spirit of God" is referred to a
number of times in the Pentateuch.

(iii) *The Detailed Statement* (verses 3–31). *Fiat Creation.*
The account given in these verses is in terms of *fiat* and *fulfilment.* The first statement is the simplest: "And God said,
Let there be light (fiat), and there was light (fulfilment)."
The Psalmist summarizes it in the words, "He spake, and
it was *done*" (Ps. xxxiii. 9). The recurring phrase, "and it
was so" (six times), is clearly emphatic. It summarizes and
forms a part of the account of the *execution* of the fiat, which
is quite as long as the fiat itself. Nothing is said as to how
it was done, about *process.* This is important. Science is concerned with material and phenomenal things, with processes
and changes, with differentiation and combination. This
account does not deny process; it ignores it. It speaks in terms
of a divine fiat, which can both use and dispense with process.
Science deals with second causes: here the First Cause is the
almighty Actor, and second causes are ignored.

The work of creation is described as taking place in six
days, each of which has an "evening and a morning".[1] The
length of these days has been much discussed. Centuries ago
Augustine declared that these days were not like our days.
Scientists, who speak in terms of light years, and add cipher
to cipher in estimating the time of the beginning of things,
ridicule the idea of twenty-four-hour days. But when they
multiply thousands to millions and millions to billions and

[1] The words "evening" and "morning" which occur in each of the six
concluding summaries are clearly emphatic. They are nearly always
used literally of our ordinary day.

billions to trillions, figures practically cease to have any meaning, and they expose their own ignorance. From the standpoint of those who believe in a God who is omnipotent, and who recognize that time and space are finite and created "things", this adding on of ciphers is absurd. It is a distinct feature of the miracles of the Bible that they are limited neither by time nor space. To "evolve" water into wine could not be done any more successfully in a million years or in a thousand million than in a "day". Natural process could not accomplish it at all. Jesus did it apparently instantaneously (John ii. 7). Did He supplement and condense natural processes, or did He dispense with them entirely?

The word "day" is used in various senses in Scripture. Exodus xx. 8–11 suggests days of twenty-four hours; but Psalm xc. 4 and 2 Peter iii. 8 declare such an inference to be unnecessary. We cannot be sure, and must not be dogmatic. We need to remember, however, that limitless time is a poor substitute for that Omnipotence which can dispense with time. The reason the account of creation given here is so simple and so impressive is that it speaks in terms of the creative acts of an omnipotent God, and not in terms of *limitless* space and *infinite* time and *endless* process.

The fact that the appearance of vegetation is assigned to the third day, and comes before the creating of sun and moon, is hard to explain. We must not suppose that the author was so ignorant of the laws of nature as not to know that the light and heat of the sun causes the grass to grow. Solar myths which connect the seasons with the birth and death of a god (e.g. Tammuz-Adonis) are very ancient. Were the account in Genesis phenomenal or mythical, it would certainly place the fourth day before the third. The explanation must lie deeper. The word "light" (verse 3) may supply the clue. If it includes the cosmic rays and other forms of radiant and atomic energy of which we are only beginning to learn the amazing potentialities, who is in a position to deny that they could have produced vegetation without or before the sun?

The now popular planetesimal or tidal theory which regards the earth as a mere by-product of the sun, produced from gases drawn forth from it by a passing star, makes tremendous demands on *time* and *chance*. There is no room for chance in a God-controlled universe. It is true that the earth is a mere speck in a universe the immensity of which we cannot grasp. But it shows very evident signs of special design. So far as we *know*, it is the only planet so constituted as to be a suitable abode for man. This makes it important; and the fact that it is the scene of man's redemption makes it of incomparably greater importance than all the other, vastly greater, heavenly bodies taken together. It is no reflection on the Genesis account to say that it is *geo*centric. It *is* geocentric, because the earth is the abode of man and the scene of his redemption, the story of which is told in the Bible.

The account of creation is definitely theistic. It speaks in terms of three great categories: God, man, nature (the phenomenal universe). God is distinct from both man and nature. He is the Creator of both. All things owe their existence to His almighty fiat. Man is distinct from God and from nature. But he is made in the image of God, and he is given dominion over the creation. He is both the climax of the creation, and a distinct creation. It is significant that "create" is used only in verse 1, of the work of creation as whole; in verse 21, of the animals; and in verse 27, of man. It occurs three times in verse 27, apparently to emphasize the unique status of man. He is the last of all the creation, and he is made in the image and likeness of God.

The law "After its kind" is to govern the propagation and increase of all the various forms of living things. It indicates that they are distinct from one another, and are to preserve their distinctness. This law, that "like begets like", is one of the most obvious *facts* of everyday experience. It has been the aim of evolutionists for many years to prove that like begets *un*like; and so to bridge all the gaps which separate the different forms of existence, one from the other, in order that all may be evolved ultimately from "protoplasm". But the gaps are still there. Naturalistic evolution is as much an "unproved hypothesis" to-day as it ever was. Those who reject the Biblical doctrine of creation are shut up to it as a "working hypothesis". But those who accept the robust theism of the Bible do not need to succumb to its spell or submit to its tyranny.

"Let us make man" (verse 26). Compare iii. 22, xi. 7. The use of the plural "us" has been explained as including the angels with God, either as consultants or agents. But the angels are nowhere mentioned in this account. It is probably best to regard this as the language of soliloquy, God talking with Himself, and as involving *in germ* the doctrine of the Trinity. But it should not be appealed to as a formal proof of it. While it has its adumbrations in the Old Testament, the doctrine of the Trinity is a New Testament doctrine. There is here no survival of a primitive polytheism, as some critics have alleged. Such a view would be quite out of harmony with the entire account which is thoroughly monotheistic.

"In our image, after our likeness": two nearly equivalent words are used to emphasize this immensely important fact. Man is made in the image and likeness of God. This sets him apart from all other creatures and entitles him to have dominion over them. He is the climax of the Creation, being brought into being last of all, in the second part of the sixth day.

"Every herb bearing seed . . . for food" (verse 30). That originally the food of man and of the animals was, and under ideal conditions will be, vegetarian is clearly taught here and suggested by Isaiah xi. 9, lxv. 25. Many of the so-called carnivora are largely or wholly vegetarians. It was after the Fall and the Flood that the eating of flesh was permitted to man.

"And behold it was very good." The satisfaction of God with His handiwork is constantly emphasized. "It was good" is stated six times; and at the end we read, "and, behold, it was very good". There was no inherent flaw or evil tendency in the creation as it came from the hands of God.

The six days of creation are followed by the day of rest. God rested from all His work. This was not the rest demanded by exhaustion. It was the complacent resting which follows a finished task. God hallowed this day as the day of His rest.

Note that this brief account omits many things. It says nothing about angels or about Satan. It leaves many questions unanswered. But it states and develops the great thesis of verse 1 in a most impressive way: "God the Creator of all things." Here the keynote of ethical monotheism is sounded which is heard throughout the whole of Scripture. This was the faith of Moses. How much of it he received by direct revelation, how much by inheritance, we do not know. It was already the faith of Abraham (xxiv. 3), and the account stands

without a peer among all the cosmogonies which have come
to us from ancient times.

It should not be necessary to repeat that this is not a tech-
nical, scientific statement. It is told in language which is
amazingly simple. It stresses the points which are especially
important; and it does this with an emphatic iteration which
is very impressive. It lays in Theism, an almighty God working by sovereign fiat, the broad and firm basis for all that
follows in Holy Writ. The aim of the above brief presenta-
tion has been primarily to point out the great and all-important emphases in this wonderful account.

The reader should not infer from the seeming simplicity of
the account of Creation that it is an easy chapter to master.
The more he studies it, the more will he be impressed with
its profundity and the variety of the questions and problems
which it raises. Thus he will note that several of the words in
this account are used in more than one sense, an ambiguity
that should be carefully noted. The "firmament" of verses
6-8, 20 appears to be the *atmosphere* which surrounds the
earth. It is also called *heaven*. But both "heaven" and "firmament" are used in verses 14-17 of the *solar* and *sidereal* heavens
which would appear to be included in the "heavens" of verse 1.
"Earth" in verses 1-2 is apparently what we call the *orbis
terrarum*; in verse 10 it is the *dry land* as distinguished from
the *seas*. "Day" in verse 5 is the *light* as distinct from the
darkness. It is used of the six creative days each of which
has an evening and a morning. In ii. 4 it comprises the whole
hexameron ("in the day that the Lord God made earth and
heaven"). "Waters" (verse 2) is used of the unorganized
matter (chaos) out of which the cosmos was formed in the
course of the hexameron. In verses 6-9 the "waters" are
divided by the firmament, and the waters below the firmament
are called *seas*.

I.—The Generations of the Heavens and the Earth (ii. 4–
iv. 26). The words of the heading, "these are the generations",
designate the section which it introduces as the first of the
ten generations of which the rest of Genesis is composed;
and the words "of the heavens and the earth" (cf. i. 1, ii. 1)
show clearly that the narrative which follows stands in close
connection with the account given in chapter i. It has three

natural divisions: (i) The Creation of Adam and Eve (ii. 4–25); (ii) The Temptation and Fall (iii. 1–24); (iii) The Immediate Consequences (iv. 1–26).

(i) *The Creation of Adam and Eve* (ii. 4–25). This account clearly presupposes the general account of creation given in chapter i, and supplements it at one point. The first account is cosmic and comprehensive. This one is detailed and particularistic. The one speaks in terms of heavens and earth, a firmament, vegetation, sun and moon, sea animals and birds, land animals, and finally of mankind in general. The second, speaking of what it calls "the generations of the heavens, and the earth", tells of a garden planted by God, of an individual man, "formed" by God and placed in the garden to till it, of the test of obedience imposed on the man and its penalty, and of the unique way in which the man was provided with a wife. The one account we might call a panorama of creation as a whole; the other a "close-up" of man, the climax of that creation. In the first account man is the cap-stone; here he is the centre.

The whole second account is, broadly speaking, an expansion or elaboration of Genesis i. 27. The planting of the garden has nothing to do with i. 11, 12. The garden is specially prepared for man. The location of the garden (ii. 10) can be determined, if at all, only through the names of the four "heads", into which it was divided. Two bear the names of well-known rivers, Hiddekel (Tigris) and Euphrates. The identification of the other two is more or less problematical. Nothing is said about a series of creative days. The statement that God formed the animals and brought them to the man to name (ii. 19 f.) serves to stress the difference between man and the lower orders. It does not conflict with the order of creation given in Genesis i. "Had formed" or "having formed" would be a perfectly proper rendering of the Hebrew.

In the passage dealing with the creation and probation of man, the dual nature of man is definitely taught. Man's body is material. It is "formed" of dust. And of this body it is said, "Dust thou *art,* and unto dust shalt thou return" (iii. 19). But into this body, Jehovah God breathed the breath of life, and man "became a living soul". How this was done we are not told. We are left in doubt whether or to what extent "formed" implies process. Physically man resembles the animals to a greater or lesser degree. But this does not prove him to be evolved from them. For the physical differences are greater and more significant than the resemblances. But it is as an intelligent, moral, spiritual being that man shows his magnificent isolation. And this he owes to the inbreathing of the Creator.

"Breathed" (verse 7), with which compares John xx. 22, seems to suggest an intimacy of relationship, which is involved in the fact that man is a "son" of God, made in His image (Luke iii. 38; Acts xvii. 28). The narrative clearly implies that man as created was capable of intimate communion with God. This must mean that God's "image" in him included such communicable attributes as "knowledge, righteousness, holiness" (Col. iii. 10; Eph. iv. 24); and the dominion over the creatures which was given him is an evidence both of his distinctness from them and of his superiority to them. They stand in the same relation to him in which he stands to God. It should be remembered, however, that the Fall made a radical change in man's status. Fallen and sinful man has no right to claim sonship to the Holy God, any more than the Jews of Jesus' day had a right to call themselves children of Abraham. They were Abraham's "seed", but not his sons. They were not sons of God, but children of the devil (John viii. 42–4). The words which are so often on the lips of Modernists and Unitarians ("the fatherhood of God and the brotherhood of man") ignore the fact of the fall of man. It was only as long as he was sinless that Adam was privileged to dwell in the garden. Expulsion from the garden (paradise) was the consequence and penalty of his alienation from God; restoration to it (Luke xxiii. 43; Rev. ii. 7) means complete restoration to sonship in the Father's house.

The fact that a very simple task is assigned the man (tending the garden) may be intended to guard against the inference that man as created was on a high cultural level (cf. Milton's *Paradise Lost*). The probation also was a very simple one, merely involving obedience to the express command of God: "And the Lord God commanded the man" (ii. 16; cf. iii. 11–17). At the very outset the proper relationship in which man stands to God is made clear. It is covered in the broadest sense by the word *command* which has as its correlative *obey*.

Thus it is made plain that man's duty is to do the will of God. As His creature, man owes his Creator willing and perfect obedience.[1] It was as a symbol and test of obedience and disobedience that the tree was "the tree of the knowledge of good and evil". It had no such qualities in itself.[2]

The account of the creation of Eve clearly teaches that the body of the first woman was formed from that of the first man. That Paul so understood it is shown by 1 Timothy ii. 13 and 1 Corinthians xi. 9, where he not merely asserts that the man was created before the woman and that the woman was created for the man, but that the woman was "of the man". This shows that Paul saw in the original creation something quite unique and highly significant. Every child of man since Adam is "born of woman" (Job xiv. 1). Eve was to be the "mother of all living" (iii. 20); but she was "of" the first man. The fact that both Jesus (Matt. xix. 4 f.) and Paul (1 Cor. vi. 16; Eph. v. 31) appeal to this narrative shows its great importance.

The woman, Adam perceives at once, is "bone of my bone". She is human, just as man is human. Hence, being created male and female, they can become "one flesh" in that conjugal relationship which God has ordained for the comfort and happiness of mankind and for the continuance of the race. Monogamy, as our Lord points out, was man's original and basic social relationship. The family is the most fundamental of the three institutions ordained by God: the family, the state, the church. Everything which invades the sanctity of the home or minimizes its importance by undermining its authority, endangers our whole Christian civilization. This is the greatest menace in Communism.

[1] It may be noted also that the word rendered "hear" in iii. 8, 10 is the same in the Hebrew as the word rendered "hearken unto" in iii. 17. This Hebrew verb occurs more than 1,000 times in the Old Testament. It is usually rendered by "hear, hearken, obey". E.g. "hear" (Deut. vi. 4), "hearken unto" (Exod. xviii. 24), "obeyed" (Gen. xxvi. 5). Consequently "hearing" ears are "obedient" ears.

[2] By this is meant that the tree may have differed from other trees only in this respect, that the prohibition attached to it made it a *moral* test. It was the tree "of" or "for" the knowing of good and evil, because eating or not eating meant obedience or disobedience to God's command. There is no reason to think that there was anything in the tree itself which had power to make them wise—that was the devil's lie (verse 5) which the woman believed.

"And they were both naked, the man and his wife, and they were not ashamed." These words prepare us for the temptation and fall, by reminding us that neither in the fact that man's body was formed of the earth and was earthly, nor in the further fact that he was created male and female, was there anything evil or that tended to evil. The whole original creation was good, very good; and man was the masterpiece of that creation.

Finally, it is to be noted that twenty times in chapters ii–iii the compound name Lord God (*Jehovah Elohim*) is used. Since this combination occurs less than twenty times in all the rest of the Old Testament, the natural explanation of its use here is that it is simply for the purpose of making plain to the reader that the God of Creation (*Elohim*) and the God of Redemption (*Jehovah*) are one and the same.

(ii) *The Temptation and Fall* (iii. 1–24). "Now (literally, 'and') the serpent." The temptation, as the sequel to the probation (ii. 17), is introduced abruptly. The serpent as the agent in the temptation is simply described as "more subtil than all the beasts of the field". Not until much later is it made clear that the real agent was Satan, the deceiver of mankind (Rev. xii. 9, xx. 2; cf. Job i. 2; John viii. 44; Rom. xvi. 20; 2 Cor. xi. 3; 1 Tim. ii. 14). Unlike the apocryphal writings of the later Jews, the Bible is extremely reticent in its treatment of supramundane matters. The revelation contained in the Bible is also progressive, and often the minimum of information is given at first and supplemented later as occasion requires.

"And she took . . . and ate." The sin was an act of disobedience. The tree and the fruit were good, the desire to be wise was good, falsehood smoothed the path. Yet it is hard to understand how a being created "good" could thus transgress a direct and express command of its Creator. Being left to the freedom of their own will, Adam and Eve fell from the estate of holiness and happiness in which they were created, into one of sin and misery. Thus early the free agency and full responsibility of man are stated, while the fact of God's sovereignty is made equally plain. But this freedom at once became bondage. "He that committeth sin is the bond-servant of sin."

Adam's sin was different from Eve's. He was present (verse 6, "with her") but he did not interpose or remonstrate. He was not deceived (1 Tim. ii. 14). But he followed Eve into an act of disobedience. In obeying his wife he disobeyed God. He loved the creature (Eve) more than the Creator. Note the terrible consequences of this act, how it affected man himself and all man's relationships; man and God (fear, flight, banishment, replace loving and reverent intimacy); man and his wife (mutual reproach, tyranny, suffering, shame, inordinate desire replace "oneness"); man and the animals (loss of dominion); man and nature (toilsome, ill-repaid labour, thorns and briars). Note how Eve first, and then Adam, seek to shift the blame for this act of sin; a very common practice that avails nothing and does not clear the guilty.

The curse pronounced on the serpent contains the first gleam of hope for mankind. The Protevangel, as it is often called (verse 15); declares that God will put enmity between the serpent and the woman for all coming generations, with the promise of victory for her seed (cf. Luke x. 18; Gal. iii. 16; Rev. xii. 9, xx. 2, 10). Here we have the beginnings of that stream of Messianic prophecy which runs through the Bible from Genesis to Revelation. Paul applies it directly to Christ. The curse on the woman is suffering and subjection; on the man toilsome and ill-requited labour, quite different from the pleasant task originally assigned him (ii. 15).

Death is the penalty of disobedience (ii. 17, iii. 19). That it means physical death is obvious, as is shown by the mournful refrain in chapter v, "and he died". But in its fullest sense death is separation and alienation from the living God. This took place at once. Expulsion from the garden, the place of communion with God, is the beginning of the carrying out of the sentence of death, by debarring him from the tree of life (verse 22). Since man was given "every tree" for food (i. 29), the tree of life may have been the one tree which fully satisfied his every physical need (cf. Rev. xxii. 2). The narrative may seem to suggest that a single partaking of the fruit of this tree would convey immortality. But this inference seems contrary to such passages as John vi. 51–9, xv. 1–14, which stress the necessity of a continuous and constant feeding and abiding. Expulsion from the garden put an end to both possibilities. Whether death applies now for the first time to the animals, which are involved in the consequences of Adam's sin (Rom. viii. 22), is not clear.

The Fall is rarely mentioned in the Bible (2 Cor. xi. 3; cf. John viii. 44). Its effects are more frequently referred to: sin, suffering, death. It is of fundamental importance to all that follows. It alone accounts for the subsequent course of the history of mankind upon the earth, for the awful contrast between i. 27, 31 and vi. 5 (cf. Rom. i. 23), and for the catastrophic course of human history which the Bible records. It represents sin as alien to man's nature as originally created; as the result of seduction from without; as something that ought not to be; as a bondage from which God purposes to redeem man. It does not, like the evolutionist, attribute it to ignorance, immaturity, limitation of being, or to the fact that man has a dual nature (body and soul). It tells us that man was created "good". Man is now a fallen being. What he needs is not merely education: he needs salvation. Only when we realize the fallen nature of man and his utter inability to save himself, are we in a position to understand the way of salvation from sin, which it is the purpose of the Bible to make known to us. The prevalent notion that children are naturally good and that all they need is to be allowed to develop in a suitable environment, that "self-expression" is to be emphasized and "correction" and "discipline" eliminated is a basic error in our modern systems of education which is responsible for much of the juvenile delinquency and crime which is a major problem to-day.

(iii) *The Immediate Consequences* (iv. 1–26). The birth of Cain and Abel was in accordance with the command given in i. 28, though affected by iii. 16 and involving the children in the sin of their parents (v. 3; cf. i. 27). The words in verse 1, "I have gotten a man with *the help of* Jehovah", seem to indicate that Eve connected the birth of Cain with the promise in iii. 15. If she hoped that Cain might be the deliverer, she was sadly disillusioned. For the prompt and awful working of sin is shown in the fact that the first child of the first pair becomes a murderer, the enemy of his fellow-men, while the last-mentioned descendant of Cain composes a hymn of hate which glories in the sin of his ancestor—a sad intimation that the day of redemption may be far removed.

Sacrifice is first mentioned here, but with no hint as to its origin. The statement that Cain and Abel both brought of their possessions might seem to imply that Cain's bloodless sacrifice would have been accepted had his spirit been right. But the prominence subsequently attached to the shedding of blood favours the view that Cain and Abel both knew (by revelation?) that a bloody sacrifice was necessary. If so, Cain's offering was rejected both because of its nature and because of the spirit in which it was offered.

"If thou doest well, shalt thou not be accepted?" (iv. 7). The meaning of the main clause is doubtful. The Revised Version has "shall it not be lifted up?" The verb means "bear, lift up, carry" and it is even used in the sense of "take away (sin)", i.e. forgive. So "acceptance, satisfaction, forgiveness" are all possible renderings. They point out the reward of virtuous conduct. The alternative, "if thou doest not well", is followed by the ominous words, "at the door sin is a croucher (a crouching beast), and toward thee is its desire (craving), but thou canst (mayest) master it (rule over it)". The figure suggests with terrible vividness the nearness, persistence, subtilty, and ferocity of the enemy of mankind (cf. 1 Pet. v. 8). Yet Cain is encouraged to believe that he may overcome. How far sin has already mastered the brute creation is shown in this figure of a wild beast crouching at the door ready to spring. How far it has mastered Cain is shown by his murder of Abel.

The question so often raised by infidels, "Where did Cain get his wife?" is sufficiently answered by v. 4. Adam was 130 years old when Seth was born. It is probable that he already had several, perhaps many, sons and daughters, and that one of the latter became Cain's wife. The mark or rather sign given Cain may have been some personal characteristic, such as a terrifying appearance or demeanour, which would cause men to fear to attack him, or perhaps some portent designed to reassure him (2 Kings xx. 8 f.).

It is noteworthy that the first mention of achievement in the arts and sciences is made in connection with the Cainites (iv. 19–22). Wickedness and inventiveness seem to have gone hand in hand. "The children of this world are wiser in their generation than the children of light." Yet mastery over the creature was God's gift to man. Lamech's song of hate and revenge highlights the wickedness of the Cainites and shows how rapidly and terribly sin corrupted the children of men.

The line of Cain is followed for seven generations and then dismissed (cf. vi. 2). With iv. 25 a new beginning is made. The "and" does not of course indicate that verse 25 follows verse 24 in order of time. It perhaps connects with verse 15 or 16. Like Eve, the name Seth is significant ("Appointed", cf. R.V. margin).

"To call on the name of Jehovah" indicates that this name of Deity, even if not often used, was known from very early times.

II.—The Book of the Generations of Adam (v. 1-vi. 8). The *second* of the "generations" begins with a brief summary based on i. 27 f. and then sums up the life of Adam in a form which serves as a pattern for the lives of his descendants. There are ten lives in this brief genealogy. The scheme is this: *x* lived —— years and begat *y*, and *x* lived after his begetting *y* —— years and begat sons and daughters; and all the days of *x* which he lived were —— years and he died. The following points are emphasized: age at parenthood, remaining years of life, birth of other children, total age, death.

The emphasis seems to be especially on the remarkable longevity of the antediluvians. This is a serious difficulty to many. It may simply mean that the deadening power of sin had not yet achieved its full effects, or struck an average, as we might say. It may also mean that these were exceptional men (cf. Moses' words in Ps. xc. 10 with Exod. vi. 16-20; Num. xxxiii. 39; Deut. xxxiv. 7; Joshua xxiv. 29), and that the average life-term before the Flood was much briefer. Besides their longevity, their fruitfulness is stressed, "and begat sons and daughters" (v. 4), and finally their death. It is to be noted that while a total of years for each life is given, there is no total given for the entire period from Adam to the Flood. This may mean that what we have here is a genealogy but not a chronology; and that links may be omitted as in many Old Testament genealogies. If so, any chronologies based on the lists in chapters v and xi may be seriously at fault.

As each life, except one, ends with the words "and he died", showing that the penalty pronounced on sin was inescapable, unless God Himself interposed (verse 24), this brief account is followed very appropriately by a statement of the terrible consequences of sin (vi. 1-8).

Genesis vi. 3 is a very difficult verse. The verb rendered "strive" (Authorised Version) may also have the meaning "rule". "Abide" (Revised margin) is favoured by LXX and Syriac, but presupposes a slightly different text. The words, "and his days shall be one hundred and twenty years", indicate that the reference is to the continued physical existence of man on earth. The meaning is either that the normal length of human life on the earth is now to be limited to 120 years or there is here a reference to the coming of the Flood which will all but destroy mankind.

The awful situation so briefly described is represented as due to intermarriage of the "sons of God" with the "daughters of men", which probably means the corrupting of the line of Seth by the line of Cain.[1]

Verses 5–8 give the most terrible picture of human degradation, to which only Romans i compares; and the strongest anthropomorphic expression is used, "and it repented the Lord", to describe God's reaction to this almost utter perversion of His creative purpose. While it is the moral effects of sin which are summarily described in these few terrible words, it is to be noted that the physical effects may have been and probably were equally marked. Sin brutalizes! Consequently it is much more in accord with the Biblical narrative to regard Neanderthal and other "primitive" forms of "man" as *degenerates* than to see in them links in a chain which derives man from lower forms of life.

Destruction of mankind is God's judgment; utter destruction, with but a single exception, "Noah found favour", is to befall the entire race of men. With this gleam of hope against a background of despair the second of the generations closes.

III.—The Generations of Noah (vi. 9–ix. 28). The third of the generations deals mainly with the Flood. Three matters are particularly stressed: (i) the sinfulness of mankind already alluded to (vi. 6–8) as the reason for the Flood. The Flood is no mere physical and natural phenomenon. It has a moral purpose. The wages of sin is death, whether the means employed to pay them be ordinary or extraordinary. God's judgments may be clear and unmistakable (Matt. xxiv. 37 f.; Luke xxi. 20 f.); they may be exemplary and men may misread

---

[1] The other view is that by "the sons of God" we are to understand "angels" (cf. Job i–ii). Whichever view is taken, it is to be remembered that this sinful race was completely destroyed by the Flood.

them (Luke xiii. 1–5; John ix. 2 f.); they may be postponed
and serve to try the faith of the righteous (Ps. xvii. 10–14,
lxxiii). But God is supremely righteous; and the Christian
should see and seek for a moral purpose in all human affairs
(Isa. xxvi. 9). (ii) The object of the Flood is "to destroy all
flesh" (vi. 7, 13, 17, vii. 4, 21–3, viii. 21). That it involved the
destruction of the human race could not be more plainly
asserted than in vii. 21–3. (iii) Grace appears in the saving of
a representative remnant of mankind, and of land animals
and birds (vi. 8, 9, 18–20, vii. 1–16, viii. 16–19).

While it cannot be asserted that the account definitely
declares the Flood to have been universal, it does describe it
as total so far as the purpose of God was concerned (note the
words "took them all away" in Matt. xxiv. 39; cf. 1 Pet. iii. 20).
Two causes of the Flood are given: the forty days of rain, and
the breaking up of the fountains of the great deep. Both are
significant. The one seems to refer to a natural phenomenon
which now manifested itself in unprecedented magnitude. But
ii. 5 is to be noted, since it may perhaps suggest that rain was
a comparatively recent phenomenon. The second factor which
was contemporaneous with the first was the "breaking up of
the fountains of the great deep" (vii. 13). This may have been
brought about by earthquakes or volcanic eruptions which
caused a sudden raising of the ocean floor; or the fall of giant
meteorites into the sea may be referred to. Immense and
various forces may be referred to in these simple words.

The evidence discovered by Woolley of a local flood in the
Euphrates valley in early times is interesting, but there is not
sufficient warrant for identifying it with the Noachic flood.
Evidences of the destructive effects of such a flood (or floods)
are found in very widely separated parts of the earth. The
fossils or frozen remains of extinct animals have been found
in Europe, Asia, Africa, and the Americas; and the condition
in which many of them have been found testifies to its sudden-
ness, and also to a change in climate, perhaps due to a sudden
shifting of the polar axis. It is important to observe that if
justice is done to the magnitude of the Flood, it may account
for many of the geological phenomena for which geologists
often demand such vast ages of time.

So much at least is certain; the Bible tells us of a flood of
incomparable destructiveness. The ancient and widespread

traditions regarding a flood confirm the Biblical statements. The best known of these is the Babylonian account, which is markedly inferior but shows certain interesting similarities.

"And Noah built an altar" (viii. 20). The first express mention of the altar refers definitely to the offering of bloody sacrifices, partly it would seem in gratitude for deliverance and also for an atonement for sin. It is followed by God's covenant promise. This involves first of all the pledge that the earth will not again be visited by a flood (verses 21 f., ix. 9–17). But there are other important features: the command to be fruitful (ix. 1, 7; cf. i. 28), dominion over the animals restored (verse 2), permission to eat meat (verse 3). It may be that this permission simply authorized a practice which had become common among the antediluvians. But we cannot infer with certainty from Abel's offering of a sacrifice that he partook of the offering. No reason is given for this permission. It would be natural to attribute it to changes in man's situation and living conditions as a result of the Flood. Whatever the reason, it clearly holds good under the New Testament dispensation (John xxi. 9; 1 Cor. iii. 2; Heb. v. 14). The permission has two important limitations: the blood is not to be eaten, and the shedding of human blood is to be punished by death. The taking of human life is so heinous a sin because man bears, even though defiled, the image of his Maker. Here we have the warrant for capital punishment (Rom. xiii. 4). The warrant for the "shall" is given in the reason annexed to the prohibition—"for in the image of God made He the man".

The sign of the covenant (ix. 13–17) is the rainbow. A better rendering of the Hebrew in verse 13 is "I have set . . . and it shall be" (cf. Revised Version). This may mean that the bow was not a new phenomenon, but that a special significance was now attached to it for the first time.

Noah "planted a vineyard . . . and he drank . . . and he was drunken . . . and he was uncovered within his tent" (ix. 20–4). This is the first mention of wine. But it seems certain that it was used by the antediluvians and that Noah was familiar with its use, wanted it, and knew how to make it. Here in a few brief and vivid words we are told of man's craving for alcohol, of the tendency to excessive use, and of its disastrous consequences: loss of self-control and of self-respect.

He "planted a vinyard" suggests a considerable interval of time and allows for the birth of Canaan and his growth to manhood (x. 1). For it is natural to assume that Canaan was implicated in the sin of his father. But no explanation of the cursing of Canaan instead of Ham is given us. So perhaps we should find here, thus early in Biblical history, a signal illustration of the fact that "no man liveth to himself". The fact that the consequences of sin often fall heavily even on the innocent should be a mighty warning and deterrent.

The blessing of Noah (ix. 25-7), like the Protevangel, makes a curse the occasion and vehicle for the pronouncing of signal blessing. The curse on Canaan is repeated three times: he is to be a servant. The blessing of Shem is enclosed in a doxology: "Blessed be Jehovah, the God of Shem." Here we have the first intimation of God's special and peculiar relationship to the line of Shem; the God of redemption is called their God (cf. Exod. iii. 6; Matt. xxii. 31 f.). In verse 27 the subject of "let him dwell" is probably "Japheth". Japheth is to be blessed through and by means of his close association with Shem. But here, as in the Protevangel, we have a striking example of the obscurity which is often characteristic of prophecy—an obscurity which is only removed either by fuller revelation of the purposes of God, or by the fulfilment of the prophecy itself in the course of history. It is to be noted that the form of the Blessing is markedly poetic. It also contains two striking word-plays: "the God (*Elohe*) of Shem" and "the tents (*ohele*) of Shem"; and "enlarge" (*yapht*) and Japheth (*yepheth*).

This one incident out of a period covering 350 years serves to remind us how much the Biblical narrative omits. Verse 28 may be regarded as completing the genealogy begun in v. 32. That Noah belongs with the antediluvians is indicated by the closing words which constitute the knell-like recurring ending of the genealogies in chapter v, "and he died".

IV.—THE GENERATIONS OF THE SONS OF NOAH (x. 1–xi. 9). The fourth of the generations gives a brief account of the descendants of Shem, Ham, and Japheth. The order is reversed, so that Japheth and Ham may be disposed of first, since Old Testament history primarily concerns the line of Shem.

Observe (i) that the list is restricted to seventy names (cf. Gen. xlvi. 27; Exod. xxiv. 1; Luke x. 1). This is clearly arbitrary, and involves the omission of names which might have been included. In the case of Japheth, seven sons and seven grandsons (children of only two of the sons) are listed. It is unlikely that five of the seven sons of Japheth were childless (cf. verses 25–9 with xi. 16–19). The data given elsewhere (e.g. xiv. 5 f., xv. 19 f.; Deut. ii. 10–12, 20–3) indicate that many other names might have been included. The reasons for some of the omissions (e.g. Sumerians, Hurrians, Kenites) and inclusions (e.g. Arvadite, Sinite, Jerah, Diklah) are not clear to us. Some of the names mentioned figure prominently in Old Testament history—e.g. Babel (Babylon), Mizraim (Egypt), Philistines—while others are only names. Archaeology has thrown considerable light on this list; and we have good reason to believe that it could have been prepared in the days of Moses. (ii) The list includes persons (e.g. Nimrod), races and nations (e.g. the -ims and the -ites). It is noteworthy that the Hamites constitute a majority, eleven descendants of Canaan being listed. (iii) The seeming identity of several names is confusing. The two Havilahs (verses 7, 29) may refer to a mingling of Hamites and Shenites. The Ludim of verse 13 are Africans, while Lud of verse 22 may denote the Lydians of Asia Minor. (iv) While the table is mainly genealogical, other factors may figure in it. Thus, the conquests of Nimrod the Hamite may have been largely over Semitic peoples, who gradually assimilated their conquerors in verse 11 read with R.V. "he (Cush) went forth into Assyria." It is to be noted that this Table of Nations precedes the account of the confusion of tongues.

The confusion of tongues (xi. 1–9) is the tragedy with which the fourth generation closes. The close connection between xi. 1 and the preceding verse indicates that it involved all of the descendants of Noah, though some would restrict it to the Shemites. The plan to build a city and a tower, and the reason assigned, "lest we be scattered abroad", would imply that this event occurred relatively soon after the Flood and before the dispersion clearly involved in chapter x (e.g. verses 10–12) took place, perhaps in the days of Peleg (x. 25; Ps. lv. 9). It is at least noteworthy and perhaps significant that here the table of the Shemites (x. 21–9) is carried in the direct line only as far as Peleg (cf. xi. 18). This, in connection with

xi. 1-4, would seem to indicate that the confusion of tongues took place in his lifetime.

It is especially important to note that the narrative does not indicate in any way that the confusion of tongues *followed genealogical or racial lines,* but rather the contrary. Thus Elam and Asshur (verse 22), sons of Shem, spoke languages which were quite different; and the same applies to Sidon and Heth (the Hittites), both sons of Canaan. This indicates that identity or similarity of language cannot be regarded as a conclusive proof of identity of race, or *vice versa.* The confusion is plainly represented as catastrophic, and attributed to the intervention of God. This will account for the racial difference between many languages and families of languages, which cannot, like simple dialectical differences, be explained as due to lapse of time and wide separation.

The name Babel is the same as Babylon (the Greek form of the word), which occurs frequently elsewhere. If the place is the same, it makes Babylon the first great centre of post-diluvial civilization. The name Babel means "gate of God" (*bab-ili*). The gate was the place of judgment; and there God confounded (*balal*) the tongues. So we have here a word-play, not an etymology. Babel does not mean "confusion".

The story of Babel suggests an important and timely question. Babel was an attempt to preserve the original oneness of mankind. But in man's fallen state it resulted in an arrogant self-sufficiency which challenged or ignored the authority of God. It was totalitarianism. To prevent this arrogance from achieving its goal, God scattered the peoples and confounded the tongues. Division and separation were necessary to prevent godless and tyrannical centralization of power in a super-state. Christianity is a truly unifying force, which transcends the barriers of nation, race, language, and temperament. But only Christianity can prevent the super-state from becoming a tyranny such as the world has never known, with a concentration of power in the hands of the few which would reduce the many to utter slavery. We may well question whether, the forces of evil, of selfishness, of cruelty, being as strong as they are, a super-state, could it be achieved, would be really desirable. One thing is certain: the League of Nations, the United Nations, and similar union movements in State and in Church, may lead, and inevitably will lead, to the enslavement rather than to the liberation of mankind, unless they are pervaded by Christian principles, which recognize and safeguard the rights of men everywhere to life, liberty, and the pursuit of true happiness, under a government which recognizes that God alone is Lord of the conscience, and that we must obey God rather than men.

V.—THE GENERATIONS OF SHEM (xi. 10–26). The fifth of the generations differs from the Table of Nations given in the fourth, by confining itself to the Shemites, and particularly to one line of descent, Shem to Abram. Like that in chapter v, it contains ten links (if following the LXX and Luke iii. 36 we insert Cainan after Arphaxad); and in both lists the last is the father of three sons (v. 32, xi. 26). This suggests that, as in Matthew i, the precise figures may be arrived at by omitting some, perhaps many, links.

It is true that many scholars (e.g. Usher) have found in these chapters the basis of an exact chronology from Adam to Abraham. But the Bible never uses them in this way; and the indefiniteness of xi. 26 would be very singular, if it concluded what was meant to be a chronology. For we would hardly infer from verse 26 that three sons were born to Terah in the same year; and comparing xi. 26, 32, xii. 4 with Acts vii. 4, we learn that Terah was 130 when Abram was born, i.e. that Abram was born sixty years after Terah became a father at seventy. Such an ending would be most unsuitable if these chapters were intended to supply the basis for an accurate chronology. One of the most noticeable differences between the two lists is that while, in Genesis v, all of the links (except Enoch) end with the mournful refrain, "and he died" (the echo of ii. 17), all of the links of Genesis xi end with the words, "and begat sons and daughters", which indicates that the command given to Noah (ix. 1) was fulfilled by his descendants.

VI.—THE GENERATIONS OF TERAH (xi. 27–xxv. 11). The sixth of the generations concerns the life of Abraham. Hence it is called "the generations of Terah", since Abraham was Terah's son. It is one of the longest, because of Abraham's prominent place in sacred history. Following his regular practice, the writer first dismisses Terah's other sons (xi.

27–32) and then passes on to narrate the career of faithful Abraham.

If we regard 2000 B.C. as an approximate date for the birth of Abraham, his life lies far within the historical period of the Ancient East as determined by historical records. If, as is generally believed, Ur of the Chaldees is the ancient Mugheir, near the head of the Persian Gulf, we now know, as a result of excavations conducted by Leonard Woolley, that its period of greatest prosperity lay a millennium before the time of Abraham. Its culture was Sumerian. Other great centres of civilization, Egypt, Assyria, Babylon, were known to him; and the incidental mention of the Hittites in chapter xxiii refers to another race which played a rôle in ancient history, the importance of which was lost sight of for centuries.

From the standpoint of ancient history, there is no reason for refusing to regard Abraham as a fully historical person. Recent discoveries at Mari indicate that Abraham lived considerably earlier than Hammurabi, who could not then be the Amraphel of Genesis xiv. But the Code of Hammurabi, even though later *in date*, represents the codification of many very ancient laws, and so throws interesting and important light on the events of Abraham's life. The same applies to other ancient documents, e.g. those from Nuzu and Mari.

The record of Abraham's life is necessarily *selective* and *episodal*. It covers a period of 100 years (xii. 4, xxv. 7); and the events which are recorded follow one another, as a rule, in chronological sequence. Abraham was seventy-five when he entered Canaan (xii. 4), eighty-six at the birth of Ishmael (xvi. 15), ninety-nine when the covenant sign was given (xvii. 1, 24), one hundred at the birth of Isaac (xxi. 2), at least 115, perhaps 125 (Josephus), when commanded to sacrifice Isaac (xxiii. 6), 137 when Sarah died (xxiii. 1; cf. xvii. 17), 140 when Isaac was married (cf. xxv. 20), 175 when he died (xxv. 7). It is to be remembered that only significant episodes are recorded. Long intervals are passed over in silence.

The call which came to Abraham was to *separate* himself. We have noted a narrowing process in the preceding chapters. Here it comes to a head. Abraham is to separate himself from his kindred. This was not accomplished by the journey to Haran. For Terah took his family thither (xi. 31), planning to go on to Canaan. Perhaps this was due to Abraham's solicitation (Acts vii. 2). If so, it was not God's plan. Haran dies in Ur. Terah dies in Haran.[1] He may have desired or consented to go to Haran because, like Ur, it was a centre of worship of the moon-god (Nannar or Sin). Cf. Joshua xxiv. 2. We are not told that Terah changed his mind and stopped half-way. The call concerned Abraham, not Terah; and God separated Abraham from both Terah and Haran by death. Nahor remained behind. Abraham took Haran's son, Lot, with him.

The blessing promised Abraham as a reward of obedience to the call to separate himself from home and kindred, is so frequently mentioned that it may be said to run like a refrain through all the story of his life. In xv. 18 and several times in chapter xvii it is called a covenant, and as such it is formally confirmed by sacrifice (xv. 9 f.) and by the sign of circumcision (xvii. 10). This blessing has three main features, each of which is mentioned repeatedly with more or less detail.

(i) The Seed (xii. 2, xiii. 16, xv. 5, xvi. 10, xvii. 2, 4–6, 16, xviii. 18, xxii. 17; cf. xxvi. 4, xxviii. 4, 14, xxxii. 12).

(ii) The Land (xii. 2, 7, xiii. 15, 17, xv. 7, 18, xvii. 8, xxiv. 7; cf. xxviii. 4).

(iii) The Nations (xii. 3, xviii. 18, xxii. 18; cf. xxvi. 4, xxviii. 14).

Abraham's life-story is a testing of his faith and obedience in respect of these three elements of the promise.

(i) *The Seed.* "But Sarai was barren; she had no child" (xi. 30). Note the emphatic tautology! Cf. xv. 2, 3, xvi. 1. This we should consider under two aspects. (a) Human expedients. (1) It seems probable that we are to infer that Abraham took Lot with him as a nephew whom he might adopt as his heir, if Sarai continued barren. His act is neither approved nor condemned. But very soon Abraham was forced to "separate himself" (note the word) from Lot; and Lot, as a kind of prodigal nephew, caused his uncle trouble and sorrow (xiv. 12 f., xviii. 23, xix. 28), and the ending of his story is humiliating and disgraceful (xix. 30–8). (2) Abraham's taking of Hagar to wife was not sinful. It was suggested by

---

[1] The name of Abraham's brother Haran is quite distinct from the name of the city of Haran (*Charran*), which apparently means "way" and describes the city as a very ancient centre of travel and traffic. The meaning of Haran is unknown.

Sarai herself: and it is not to be forgotten that the promise that Sarai should herself bear the child who is to be Abram's heir is not given until after the birth of Ishmael. This proposal was fully in accord with custom and law as Abraham knew it. But it was not in accord with the ideal of marriage (ii. 23 f.). It was not God's plan. It led to presumption, jealousy, cruelty, and finally to enforced *separation* of Abraham from his son Ishmael. (*b*) God's Purpose. "Sarah thy wife shall bear thee a son" (xvii. 19), "in Isaac shall thy seed be called" (xxi. 12). Abraham's faith was severely tested regarding this promise: (1) By delay which made its fulfilment humanly impossible (xviii. 14; Rom. iv. 19; Heb. xi. 11), the very idea ridiculous (xvii. 17, xviii. 12, xxi. 6). So a great feast celebrated the fulfilment of the promise (xxi. 8). (2) By the command to sacrifice the child of destiny: "Thy son, thine only son, Isaac, whom thou lovest" (xxii. 2)—every word a stab! Note the words, "Behold, here am I" (verses 1, 7, 11; cf. especially xxxvii. 13; 1 Sam. iii. 4; Isa. vi. 3). It is the expression of ready response and obedience; even used by God of Himself (Isa. lii. 6, lviii. 9, lxv. 1). The son who is the promised seed, for whose sake Ishmael has been sent away, is now to be given back to God in sacrifice. This is the supreme test of Abraham's faith. The story is told with extreme reticence and delicacy, solely in terms of "the obedience of faith". We are left to picture the anguish of the father's heart. Jephthah's lament is recorded (Judges xi. 35). Abraham's is passed over in silence as a sacred thing too deep for sighs or tears. We are not even told whether Abraham told Sarah either before or afterwards. The only hint given us regarding Isaac's attitude, apart from his apparent passivity, is in the expressive words used by Jacob regarding his father's God, "the Fear of Isaac" (xxxi. 42), which may suggest the awe with which this terrible experience of his youth led Isaac to speak of the God of his father Abraham. The words, "I and the lad will go yonder . . . and come again to you", have been regarded as deceitful, as meaning that if he gave his servants a hint of his purpose they might try to prevent its accomplishment. But the only explanation worthy of the incident as a whole is that Abraham believed that God, who had given Isaac to him, would in some mysterious way restore this child of promise to him; and this is the interpretation given us in Hebrews xi. 19. Observe that the words, "the Lord will provide" (verse 8), are in Hebrew "Jehovah jireh" (verse 14). (3) Abraham's concern for a righteous seed gives us one of the most beautiful incidents of the Old Testament, the story of the securing of a wife for Isaac. It was of vital concern to Isaac. But it is told as the expression of the obedient faith of his father, which required separation from the people of the land. The fidelity of the servant is beautifully described. If he is that Eliezer of Damascus (xv. 2) whom Abraham at one time regarded as his heir, this story shows him to have been the true child of Abraham's faith, a faith which received an immediate and abundant answer (verses 14, 17–20, 43–6). The kindly and obliging spirit of Rebekah, and her youthful vigour (she drew water for ten thirsty camels), are a part of the test. Being beautiful and eminently desirable, she was probably quite young, twenty or even twenty-five years younger than Isaac. (4) The long period of Rebekah's barrenness (twenty years, xxv. 26) was a further element, perhaps the final one, in the testing of Abraham's faith regarding the seed. Abraham was 160 years old when Rebekah gave birth to the twins, Esau and Jacob.

The marriage with Keturah is the strangest incident in the long life of Abraham. No explanation is given. It is recorded with utmost brevity and objectivity. We may not assume that it was a kind of repetition of the Hagar-Ishmael expedient, undertaken because of Rebekah's barrenness. For Abraham knew definitely that "in Isaac shall thy seed be called". It is probable that, with Isaac safely married and "comforted" after his mother's death, Abraham in his loneliness took another wife, while at the same time making provision that Isaac should be his heir (xxv. 5). The thirty-five years after Sarah's death would give ample time for the birth of sons and even grandsons. So it is not necessary to infer that Abraham married Keturah before the death of Sarah, though this possibility is not to be overlooked. Unlike Hagar, Keturah is never mentioned in the New Testament.

(ii) *The Land.* "Unto thy seed will I give this land" (xii. 7). The promise of the land tested Abraham's faith to the very end of life. (a) He was a sojourner (*ger*) in it (xii. 10, xvii. 8, xx. 1, xxi. 23 f., xxiii. 4; cf. xxxv. 27). "By faith he sojourned in the land of promise as in a strange country" (Heb. xi. 9) sums it up graphically. (b) The land was in the possession of others.

It was called Canaan (xi. 31); and the Canaanites (xii. 6; cf. x. 18 f.) and other nations, to the number of ten (xiii. 7, xv. 18–21) were in possession of it. (*c*) He was twice driven out of it by famine (xii. 10–20, xx. 1–18), and involved in difficulties and dangers which made him keenly conscious of his "pilgrim" state on the earth (Heb. xi. 13). (*d*) The land was invaded by foreign foes, and he became involved because of Lot (xiv. 1–28). (*e*) Abraham was obliged to *buy* a burial-place in it where he might "bury my dead out of my sight" (xxiii. 8). This is the most pathetic scene, as that on Mount Moriah is the most tragic, in the life of Abraham.

(*iii*) *The Nations.* "In thee shall all families of the earth be blessed" (xii. 3). Here again the very incongruity of his situation tested his faith. (*a*) His sojourns in Egypt (xii) and in Gerar (xx) brought affliction on these "nations" and danger to himself because of his deceit and lack of faith. (*b*) He had to fight with invading armies to save Lot, his only kin this side of Haran, from being carried away captive by them (xiv). (*c*) His intercession for Sodom was unavailing (xviii–xix). (*d*) His neighbours took away his wells (xxi. 24 f.).

Separation, not only from the "nations" but even from his next of kin, Nahor, Lot, Ishmael, Keturah's sons, was the requirement. Yet in him and his seed all the nations were to be blessed.

In view of the testing of Abraham's faith by the disparity and incongruity between the promise and the reality, we naturally ask ourselves whether and to what extent the promise has been fulfilled.

(*i*) *The Seed.* Notice (*a*) The Numerous Seed. Cf. Exodus xii. 37; Numbers xxii. 11; 1 Kings iv. 20; 1 Chronicles xxvii. 23. These verses, especially the last two, which clearly echo the words of the promise, indicate that certainly in the days of David and Solomon the promise of the numerous seed had had a glorious fulfilment. (*b*) The Unique Seed. Galatians iii. 16 states definitely what the whole course of Messianic prophecy makes plain, that the Seed in whom the nations are to be blessed is Christ. When Abraham saw His day (John viii. 56), he saw the promise fulfilled.

(*ii*) *The Land.* (*a*) In Old Testament times. Compare 1 Kings iv. 21 with Genesis xv. 18–21, which shows that the promise was then fulfilled, although the possession was later forfeited through unbelief and disobedience. (b) According to Prophecy. Cf. Psalms ii, lxxii; Isaiah ii. 2, lvi. 7.

(iii) *The Nations*. (a) The Old Testament period was markedly particularistic. Israel was a separate and separated people. Her dealings with foreign nations, and dependence on them for help, are often denounced by the prophets. E.g. Isaiah xxx. 2; Jeremiah xlii. 13–17; Ezekiel xvi and xxiii. (b) The universal note appears strongly in prophecy. E.g. Psalms lxxii, cxvii; Isaiah ii. 2–5, xix. 23–5; Joel ii. 28–32. (c) In New Testament times the existence of the Jewish *diaspora* was, and had been for centuries, a leavening force throughout the Greco-Roman world (Acts ii. 5–11). (d) The Great Commission (Matt. xxviii. 18–20) makes the Kingdom of Messiah, Abraham's Seed, world-wide. Barriers of territory, race, nation, colour, are all done away. All nations are to be blessed through the proclamation of the Gospel of Jesus the Christ, who is the Son of David, the Son of Abraham, the Son of God.

Abraham is one of the greatest figures in redemptive history. In the New Testament he is mentioned about as often as Moses. He is the great embodiment of faith, a faith which found expression in obedience (Rom. iv; Gal. iii; Heb. xi. 8–19). That this faith involved and rested on knowledge greater than the meagre record before us would lead us to infer, is indicated by such passages as John viii. 56 and especially Mark xii. 24–7. Abraham's conduct on Mount Moriah would be inexplicable had his view-point been that of 1 Corinthians xv. 32b. Jesus set the faith and obedience of Abraham in marked contrast with the blindness and disobedience of his unworthy "children" (John viii. 39). Note the importance of casual statements. Abraham was called to a separated life. But Abraham had 318 "trained men, born in his house"—a household of perhaps 1,000 souls (cf. Gen. xxvi. 16).

Attempts have been made to disprove the historicity of Abraham, to dissolve him in a myth; a legend, an eponymous hero of a tribe. But, except to those who deny the supernatural, the figure of Abraham is wonderfully real and life-like, and it is placed in a setting the historical accuracy of which is increasingly established by archaeological research. He is a very human figure, and his faults are not concealed from us. But he is also a heroic figure, and his life of faith makes him a pattern for all generations to come (Heb. xi). The final verdict is given by God Himself in these wonderfully impressive words, which give the reason for the confirming of the covenant to Isaac: "Because that Abraham obeyed My voice, and kept My charge, My commandments, My statutes, and My laws" (xxvi. 5). And his obedience was the obedience of faith. For this reason he is referred to by Paul as "faithful Abraham" (Gal. iii. 9); and in both Testaments he is called the "friend of God" (2 Chron. xx. 7; Isa. xli. 8; James ii. 23), a unique distinction, yet one to which our Lord admits all His faithful followers (John xv. 13 f.).

VII.—THE GENERATIONS OF ISHMAEL (xxv. 12–18). The death of Abraham having brought Isaac and Ishmael together (verse 9) leads quite naturally to the seventh of the generations, which deals with and disposes of Ishmael. Verse 16 reminds us how faithful God is in the fulfilling of His promises (xvii. 20). No further mention of Ishmael is made except incidentally (xxviii. 9, xxxvi. 3, xxxvii. 25 f., xxxix. 1). Yet the mention of Ishmael's age at his death (137 years) and the use of the unusual words "gave up the ghost", serve to emphasize the fact that he was a son of Abraham (cf. xxv. 8, 17, xxxv. 29, xlix. 33) and the heir of a promise of blessing (xvii. 20). But xvi. 12 is also needed to complete the picture.

VIII.—THE GENERATIONS OF ISAAC, ABRAHAM'S SON (xxv. 19–xxxv. 29). The form of this heading indicates that the eighth of the generations has to do not with Isaac primarily, but with Isaac's sons, Esau and Jacob. The omission of a heading, "these are the generations of Abraham", is significant. For such a heading would introduce a section dealing with Isaac. But Isaac is in a very real sense only the connecting link between his father Abraham and his son Jacob. Hence his own life-story comes partly under the "generations of Terah", which concern Abraham, and partly under the "generations of Isaac", which concern Isaac's sons. The reason for this is that the main interest in Isaac's career, after his marriage (xxiv), centres in the fact that he becomes the father of twins. Which of them is to inherit the blessing? This is the great problem of Isaac's later life. And it is told in the "generations of Isaac".

The interval (twenty years) between Isaac's marriage at forty (xxv. 20) and the birth of the twins (verse 26) was a test of Isaac's faith. Their birth was in answer to his prayer (xxv. 21). But it was accompanied by experiences sufficiently disquieting to cause Rebekah to "inquire" of the Lord. This probably means that she went to the place of sacrifice where God had appeared to Abraham and to Isaac; and there God spoke to her—whether by an audible or inner voice, whether in dream or vision or theophany, we are not told. The word spoken to her is cast in poetic parallelism, and the language is more or less obscure:

"Two nations (are) in thy womb,
  And two peoples from thy bowels shall be separated:
  And (the one) people shall be stronger than (the other)
    people
  And great shall serve little."

Two things are to be noted regarding this rather enigmatic oracle: (i) It speaks mainly in terms of races and nations, not of individual persons; only in the last line, *if at all*, does it refer directly to Esau and Jacob; (ii) the last line is ambiguous, because in the Hebrew either "great" or "little" can be regarded as the subject of "serve". That is, the renderings, "great shall serve little" and "little shall serve great" are both possible.[1] These points are to be carefully noted, in view of the attitude taken by Isaac and Rebekah to the problem of the succession. It is this ambiguity which makes this oracle a moral test, by making it possible for Isaac and Rebekah to differ as to its meaning.

Verses 27–34 cover the period of the early life of the twins. The vital problem is introduced in verse 28: *Isaac* loved *Esau, Rebekah* loved *Jacob*. One reason and only one is given for Isaac's preference for Esau, "he did eat of his venison". For Rebekah's preference no reason is stated. Thus the stage is set for the struggle that is inevitable. A significant incident, the sale of the birthright, is mentioned, partly with a view to prepare us for it. The birthright was apparently the right of the firstborn to headship in the family or tribe and probably also to a double portion of the inheritance

---

[1] For a detailed discussion of this passage, see "The Birth Oracle to Rebekah" by the present writer (*Evangelical Quarterly*, 1939, pp.97–117).

(Deut. xxi. 17; 2 Kings ii. 9). The characters of the brothers are clearly revealed by this telling incident: the reckless improvidence and carnality of Esau, the scheming selfishness of Jacob. The blessing meant nothing to Esau; he sold it for a mess of pottage.

With Isaac, as with his father, God's personal and intimate dealings are of prime importance, but here (xxvi), as in chapters xii, xiv, xx, wider contacts of the life of the patriarch are described. Isaac's faith is tried by famine (cf. xii. 10) and not being permitted to go down into Egypt, he goes to Gerar. Like his father, he appears there in an ignoble light, and is forced to separate himself. Abimelech's words, "Go from us, for thou art mightier than we" (verse 16) may indicate that at this time there were relatively few Philistines in the land and that their main migration came later. Isaac, like Abraham, failed conspicuously to be a blessing to the nations.

At the age of forty, which was Isaac's age when he married Rebekah, Esau took two Hittite wives. Since they were probably native women, marriage with whom was particularly to be avoided (xxiv. 3), this act was defiant, and the fact that the marriage was or soon became polygamous made it doubly offensive. Why did Isaac make no effort, apparently, to forestall or prevent it? The grief of mind of both parents is recorded; and that is all.

Man Proposes and God Disposes. Compare xxvii. 1–4 with xxiv. 1 f. Abraham was about 140 years old when he secured a wife for Isaac. Isaac is now nearly as old, about 137.[1] Abraham had thirty-five years to live; Isaac has about forty-three. Yet they both act as if death may be very near. But how different are the scenes! Esau has now been married nearly forty years, and has sons and probably grandsons, half-Hittite. Jacob is still unmarried, though nearly eighty, and Isaac has done nothing about it. This must mean that he

[1] This figure is arrived at in the following way. Joseph was thirty when he interpreted Pharaoh's dream (xli. 46). He was thirty-nine (seven years of plenty and two of famine, xlv. 6) when Jacob came to Egypt at the age of 130 (xlvii. 6). Consequently Joseph was born when his father was ninety-one. Since this was at the end of fourteen years of service under Laban, Jacob must have been about seventy-seven when he left home, which would make Isaac about 137. It is, of course, to be remembered that the 130 years mentioned by Jacob may be a rough number.

regards Esau as his heir, and perhaps considers Jacob's bachelorhood favourable to his plans. His love for Esau is of long standing. Esau has been his purveyor of venison. "Esau" has spelled "venison" to Isaac. And now, expecting death, he wants one more dish of Esau's venison, such as he loves, that he may bless Esau. What a contrast with chapter xxiv! And he means to perform this solemn act secretly, by stealth. This, and Rebekah's conduct, show that the struggle is primarily one between the parents, and it suggests that Rebekah has been expecting such a move and preparing to frustrate it. The means employed, the savoury food, the skins, the raiment, show her quick-wittedness and forethought (cf. 1 Kings i; Matt. xx. 20–8). Rebekah's tricks lead to Jacob's lies, and to the crowning infamy, the Judas kiss (verse 27).

It is instructive to compare the three blessings in the light of the Abrahamic covenant. (i) The first (verses 27–9) is markedly coloured by the fact that Isaac intends it for Esau, though it has elements of the covenant promise in it. The words, "thy mother's sons" (verse 29), sound almost spiteful and vindictive. Jacob has been a "mother's boy" all these years; and Isaac has resented it. Now at last he will have his way. He has apparently convinced himself that the birth-oracle permits him to bless Esau. So the discovery that he has been tricked is overwhelming, especially because he at once recognizes the hand of God in it (verse 33). (ii) The second blessing is Esau's own; and it follows very closely the language of the first, which Isaac had meant for him. It is granted because of Esau's wrathful and sorrowful protest and appeal. "For he hath supplanted me" (verse 36) might be paraphrased "For he hath Jacobed me". Jacob means "heeler" (xxv. 26) or "supplanter", and the verb comes from the same root. Note the ambiguity of the "of" (verse 39), which may be rendered "away from" (Revised Version margin). It does not withdraw but repeats the declaration that he shall serve his brother, but it declares that this servitude shall have an end (verses 39, 40). (iii) The third blessing (xxviii. 3, 4) is the true Abrahamic blessing, and refers to both the seed and the land. That it says nothing of the nations need not surprise us. Isaac has at last acquiesced in what he now knows to be the will of God; and he constitutes Jacob the full heir of the promise and sends him away to Haran to secure a wife from his mother's family. So the story of this domestic struggle ends with Jacob fleeing from the threatened vengeance of Esau, and Esau taking two more wives (daughters of Ishmael), whether as an act of bravado or of compromise we cannot say (xvii. 20). It is a sad and even sordid story of domestic strife which has found its counterpart throughout the centuries in many homes.

It is noteworthy that while Isaac "entreated" the Lord because of Rebekah's barrenness, and Rebekah "inquired" of Him when her hour was approaching, we are not told that either Isaac or Rebekah sought divine guidance in dealing with the all-important question of the blessing. They consulted rather their own personal likings and preferences. Nevertheless, God's purpose was accomplished. Jacob received the Abrahamic blessing. So now Isaac and Rebekah practically disappear from the stage. Rebekah sends Jacob away for "a few days". Whether she ever saw him again we do not know. After twenty years in the far country Jacob steals away "to go to Isaac his father in the land of Canaan" (xxxi. 18). Yet it is perhaps significant that the account of Jacob's actual meeting with his father is immediately followed by the account of Isaac's death (xxxv. 27–9).

It is to be noted that in Hebrews xi. 20 Isaac's blessing of Jacob and Esau is described as an act of faith. This statement might be regarded as applying only to the second and third of the blessings, which were uttered after he realized, through the thwarting of his plan to bless Esau, that it was God's will to bless Jacob. But the first blessing could perhaps be called an act of faith if Isaac really believed, or had persuaded himself, that the birth-oracle gave the preference to Esau. It is rather remarkable that Esau is expressly included with Jacob: "By faith Isaac blessed Jacob and Esau, even concerning things to come."

From this point on, Jacob occupies the centre of the stage. From Beersheba to Bethel (Luz) is about forty-five miles as the crow flies, but through hilly country. If Jacob reached it in a single day, it shows his eagerness to escape from Esau's vengeance (xxxv. 1). Reaching Luz after its gates were closed, he slept in the open field. It was God's appearing to him which made the place sacred. He "dreamed"; and in the dream the God of his fathers confirms the covenant to him, with especial reference to his journey and sojourn away from home. Jacob is deeply impressed. Yet he answers God's gracious promise with an "if" which sounds somewhat churlish and sceptical. If God will do His part, I will do mine! Jacob seems to be surer of himself than he is of God. It is the dream which sanctifies both place and stone for Jacob. He set up the stone to mark the place, poured oil over it as a libation, vowed that on his safe return he would make it a sanctuary, and that there he would pay tithes (cf. xiv. 20). Later, when about to leave Haran, the God of Bethel appears to Jacob (xxxi. 13) commanding him to return to the land of his kindred, and still later Jacob is commanded to go to Bethel and "make an altar" (xxxv. 1). He called this altar "El-beth-El" (the God of Beth-el), which clearly refers us to xxviii. 22. But nothing is said about the "stone" or "pillar".

The meeting with Rachel is affecting, but is in marked contrast with the servant's meeting with Rebekah (xxiv. 27 f.). Jacob seems unconscious of divine guidance here, nor when Laban tricks him into marrying Leah is there any remorse mingled with his indignation, because of the trick he had played on his blind father (both deeds of darkness) not so long before as to be easily forgotten. "Fulfil her week" refers clearly to the week of the wedding feast (Judges xiv. 12). The word "week" is especially significant for its bearing on Genesis ii. 2, since it implies that a seven-day week was familiar to the patriarchs. After the feast is ended Jacob receives Rachel. Thus he serves fourteen years for his two wives, and receives both of them at the beginning of the eighth year. In marrying the two handmaids he follows Abraham's example, without Abraham's excuse.

The narrative clearly indicates that eleven children were born to Jacob during the second seven years. After Joseph's birth at the end of this period (xxx. 25), Jacob wishes to leave; but Laban prevails on him to remain, and Jacob makes a bargain that is so seemingly disadvantageous that Laban accepts it (xxx. 31–4), but changes it ten times with a view to his own advantage (xxxi. 41). That Jacob believed in pre-natal influence is clearly indicated. But note that (i) Jacob does not attribute the stratagem of xxx. 37–42 to God, but only the plan itself as outlined in verses 31–4, with which compare xxxi. 10–13; (ii) this clever device could not account for Jacob's unbroken success (xxxi. 8); (iii) Jacob definitely attributes his success to God (xxxi. 5, 9). The means to which Jacob resorted to secure the fulfilment of the dream may have been quite as unnecessary to the fulfilment of God's purpose as was Abraham's marriage with Hagar. Consequently, this incident should not be appealed to as proof that the Bible supports the theory of pre-natal influence, which has often caused mothers needless anxiety and is not accepted by many or most medical men to-day.

The distance from Haran to Gilead is some 300 miles; and for Jacob, travelling with flocks and herds, it was a slow and tedious journey. For a group of men mounted on camels or swift asses a very much shorter time would be needed. So verse 23 need not mean that Laban started immediately in pursuit. Laban knew how slowly Jacob must travel, and that he could easily overtake him.

The meeting of Jacob and Laban is a kind of diamond-cut-diamond affair. All the bottled-up bitterness in Jacob's heart is poured out now. Laban makes it plain that fear of God's vengeance alone restrains him from the use of violence. His attempt to put Jacob in the wrong (verses 26–30) is so over-done that it makes him ridiculous, and makes Jacob righteously indignant. The "images" (teraphim, xxxi. 19, 34) are called "gods" in verses 30, 32. This incident shows that Jacob has been living in an idolatrous environment (xxxv. 2; Joshua xxiv. 15). To what extent he has himself been influenced by it we cannot say (verse 32). The "twenty years" referred to in verses 38 and 41 seem to refer to the same period, the second statement being more detailed than the first.[1]

---

[1] Some scholars hold that two periods of twenty years are spoken of: the period of service for hire (fourteen years for the two wives; six years for the cattle) which is definitely summarized in verse 41 as totalling twenty years, and a second period of twenty years of "unpaid service" referred to in verse 38. It goes without saying that this would relieve the difficulty of crowding so many events into the second seven years (xxix. 27). But xxx. 25 f. certainly implies that the agreement to serve for the cattle followed at once on the completion of the term of service for the wives. To insert an interval of twenty years, beginning either before or after the birth of Dan and Naphtali and to place the birth of Joseph at the close of this twenty years, is decidedly arbitrary. It is also difficult to account for Jacob's willingness to serve Laban for twenty years simply for "maintenance" ("was I in thy house"). But this interpretation is ably defended in the Ellicott and Speaker's Commentaries.

The covenant (verses 43–54) is one between enemies, not friends. God is to "watch" between Jacob and Laban lest either should harm the other. In the Mispeh Benediction it is given a quite different meaning. The mention of the "Syriac" (Aramaic) name for "heap of witness" as used by Laban adds vividness to the story and we are told repeatedly that Laban was a "Syrian" (xxv. 20, xxviii. 5, xxxi. 20, 24; cf. esp. Deut. xxvi. 5). The heap and the pillar are to serve as a boundary between Laban and Jacob; and this agreement is ratified by a sacrificial meal.

"The Angels of God" (xxxii. 1): in the Hebrew the same word (*mal'ak*) is used for a superhuman and a human "messenger". So the rendering "angels" interprets it in the former sense. Mahanaim ("two camps") may refer to the angelic host and Jacob's host. But cf. verses 7, 10.

We now come to the Meeting with Esau (xxxii. 3–xxxiii. 17). First Laban, now Esau! Conscience makes cowards of us all! Years of separation have not dissipated Jacob's fear of Esau. Jacob's prayer (verses 9–12) shows us a different Jacob, a man conscious of his unworthiness, weakness, and need of divine help. Yet the almost grovelling servility with which he addresses Esau as "my lord" shows how little confidence he places in the birthright which he had stolen or in the blessing that he had received, or else that he did not apply the blessing to himself personally. No reason is given for Esau's cordiality, in marked contrast to Laban's peaceableness, which we are told was due to fear of God only. Yet Jacob cannot be frank and open with Esau. Apparently Jacob never went to Seir (xxxiii. 14).

The Wrestler at Jabbok (xxxii. 22–32) is described as "a man", but cf. verse 30 and Hosea xii. 4. The mighty power of this Being (an angel, or the Angel of the covenant) is shown by the fact that he has only to "touch" Jacob's thigh to maim him. Yet he asks Jacob to let him go, and allows Jacob to prevail and obtain a blessing from him. This perhaps explains the name "Israel", which apparently means "God persists or prevails". Yet the explanation given elsewhere is "for thou as a prince (*sar*) hast persisted with God and with men, and hast prevailed" (verse 28; cf. Hos. xii: 4 f.). God prevails, yet He also permits His children to prevail with Him!

"Not Jacob any more, but Israel." It is singular that the same command is given a second time (xxxv. 10). Still more remarkable is it that both names continue to be used throughout the Old Testament and also in the New Testament. This seems to mean that the significance does not lie in the mere names but in their meaning. Jacob the scheming "heeler" is to become "Israel", who prevails with God, but only when God prevails with him. Yet Israel is the name appropriated by the Northern Kingdom, which was characterized by apostasy!

"And Jacob came (to) Shalem" (xxxiii. 18). Three meanings of *shalem* are possible: "to Salem", the name of a town; "in peace"; or "in health", i.e. healed of his lameness. The second seems preferable. "And he bought the (not 'a') parcel of the field" (verse 19) suggests that the sojourn at Shechem was quite an extended one.

The Dinah Incident (xxxiv)—an instructive but unsavoury story—pictures Jacob as, probably because of age, no longer master in his own house, and his sons as deceitful and cruel. Simeon and Levi, whatever their age, were probably assisted by some of their father's herdsmen and other servants in carrying out their treacherous and vindictive design.

The Return to Bethel (xxxv. 1–15). How soon this followed the blood-bath at Shechem we cannot say. Verse 5 suggests a close connection. Jacob calls on his household to forsake idolatry, and the Lord appears to him and blesses him in terms of the covenant (verses 9–15). Certain incidents of moment are briefly recorded: the death of Deborah, whose name is mentioned here, though not in xxiv. 59; the death of Rachel in giving birth to Benjamin; and finally, Reuben's unfilial conduct.

The mention of the birth of Benjamin (verses 16–26) leads naturally to the giving of a complete list of all of Jacob's sons (verses 22–6), with mention of the names of their mothers. Here for the first time the number twelve can be used of them. Ishmael was to beget twelve princes, and Jacob now has twelve sons. The death of Isaac (verses 27–9) must have occurred about twenty years after the birth of Benjamin, and about a dozen years after Joseph was sold into Egypt. The fact that Isaac's death is mentioned immediately after "Jacob came unto Isaac his father unto Mamre" may mean that the two events were closely connected in time, that Isaac never saw Jacob again, after he sent him away to Haran, until nearly the time of his death. But it is also possible that a period of some years is passed over here in silence as is not seldom the case in Biblical narratives. Nothing remains to be told us of Isaac's career, and the record is completed by this brief record of his death. The statement that "Esau and Jacob his sons" (note the order, Esau put first) buried him is noteworthy and prepares for the Generations of Esau which immediately follow it.

The story of Jacob is not yet ended. But from now on he plays but a minor rôle in the amazing story of his son Joseph, the hero of the last of the Generations. The story as told us thus far is not an inspiring one. Jacob, like his father Isaac, is a very different man from his grandfather Abraham. In the case of Abraham we almost forget his faults as we contemplate that wonderful obedience of faith which was tested and purified in the furnace of frustration and trial. In Isaac we have a man whose only mission in life was to pass on the heritage of promise which he had received, and who, but for the sovereign grace of God, who can make even the wrath of men to praise Him, would have utterly failed to carry out the purpose of God. In the career of Jacob up to this point we see a selfish, worldly schemer, whose faults are so apparent that his virtues are largely obscured by them.

IX.—The Generations of Esau (xxxvi. 1–xxxvii. 1). Before the story of Genesis reaches its conclusion in the career of Joseph, the descendants of Esau must be mentioned and dismissed. This is the ninth of the Generations. It is significant that it is divided into two parts, which might be called "Esau in Canaan" (cf. verses 5–7) and "Esau in Edom" (verses 8–43). Verse 31 has been regarded as requiring a date for this record much later than the time of Moses. But it is to be remembered that the kingship was definitely foretold long before it was established (Gen. xvii. 6, 16; Deut. xvii. 14–20). In describing the regal power of Edom, Moses might well point out that in contrast the royal period in Israel was still future. Some scholars who hold to the Mosaic authorship of the Pentateuch think a few names may have been added to these lists at a later date. But we know nothing as to the length of reign of these Edomite kings.

X.—THESE ARE THE GENERATIONS OF JACOB (xxxvii. 2–l. 26). The last of the generations in Genesis deals chiefly with Joseph, the most distinguished of Jacob's sons. This is indicated by the fact that Joseph is immediately introduced, and in what follows we have the story of his life from his seventeenth year to his death ninety-three years later. Jacob's other sons, and Jacob himself, play quite secondary rôles.

The events which led up to the first great crisis in Joseph's life are briefly told: Joseph's tale-bearing, Jacob's partiality which led to jealousy and hate, Joseph's dreams, the perhaps boastful and premature telling of which caused even his father to reprove him[1]—all these things added fuel to the flames. Everything points to trouble. Yet Jacob acts with almost criminal stupidity. He knows of the jealousy between Leah and Rachel, he knows only too well the cruel and ruthless temper of two of Leah's sons and the reckless spirit of the oldest of them. He has himself added fuel to the flames by making Joseph his pet. Yet he sends him, a lad of seventeen, apparently alone, on a journey of more than fifty miles, to inquire how his brethren are faring; sends him to Shechem, where Jacob's name had been made a stench (xxxiv. 30) because of the inhumanity of Simeon and Levi.

Jacob's guilelessness is hard to understand, for Jacob was by no means a guileless individual. He loves Joseph. Yet he delivers him into the hands of his brothers, and by so doing he exposes them to a temptation too great for them to resist. And Joseph does his full part. With youthful *insouciance* or braggadocio, he wears his "coat of many colours", the hated symbol of their father's preferment, so that they see and recognize him afar off (verse 18); like a "red rag" it arouses their anger and dares them to do their worst. If this coat was, as some think, a garment with long sleeves and reaching to the feet, it was eminently inappropriate for such a journey.

---

[1] Jacob's words, "I and thy mother and thy brethren" may have been meant to point out the absurdity of the dream, since Rachel had been dead for many years. If so, Jacob took the dream too literally. Yet he was impressed by it. For we are told that he "observed" it (i.e. bore it in mind and remembered it).

If Joseph expected his brethren to receive him as their father's messenger and "bow" to him, he sadly misjudged them.

Three proposals indicate their state of mind: (i) To slay him, cast him into a pit, say a wild beast devoured him (murder, concealment, falsehood): a heartless proposal on which most were ready to act at once (verse 21). (ii) To cast him into a pit "in the desert", to die of hunger and thirst as in the *oubliette* of a medieval castle (murder by indirection, "let not our hand be upon him"). Reuben's proposal (verse 22), had it been sincerely meant (cf. verse 29, also xlii. 22), would have been even more inhuman than the first. No wonder it was accepted! (iii) To sell him to the Ishmaelite-Midianites. Judah's proposal is at least an improvement on the other two. Judah perhaps went as far as he dared. But the danger and folly of compromising with evil is illustrated by the outcome. Joseph's life was spared, only for him to become a slave. The cowardly and cold-blooded method of breaking the news to Jacob shows the extent of their hate: Jacob must be convinced that his favourite son is *dead*. Their cruelty is only matched by their hypocrisy, their attempts to "comfort" their father. This story casts a lurid light upon the character of most of the ancestors of the twelve tribes of Israel. It ends with Joseph a slave in Egypt. The brothers had accomplished their fell purpose!

Chapter xxxviii gives us a glimpse into the family life of Judah, the founder of the royal tribe. The words "at that time" connect the events to be described with the preceding incident. Perhaps Judah could not stand for long the sight of his father's grief and keep up the rôle of hypocrite imposed by his own wrongdoing. So he goes off by himself and marries a daughter of the land. The narrative covers some twenty years (xlvi. 12) and does no credit to Judah. Yet it is needed to trace the descent through Judah. The Tamar incident shows that Levirate marriage (Deut. xxv. 5) was an ancient custom. The deception practised by Tamar on Judah indicates how greatly Judah's moral fibre had deteriorated, how greatly he had been influenced by the customs of the Canaanites among whom he had been living for a score of years. For the word "harlot" (verse 15, *kedeshah*, "devotee") implies that Tamar disguised herself with a view to being taken, not for a woman of the street, but for a "religious prostitute". This means that Judah did not scruple to practise one of the abominations of the heathen which shows us the worship of the Canaanites at its worst. Apparently Tamar, like Shuah, was a Canaanitess. It is significant that Tamar is mentioned in the genealogy in Matthew i—Tamar, Rahab, Ruth, Bathsheba. Having completed this account of Judah's doings by bringing it down to about the time of Jacob's descent into Egypt, the story of Joseph is resumed.

The events described in chapters xxxix and xl cover a period of about ten years (xli. 1, 46) and show us Joseph tested in the school of adversity. The writer directs particular attention to the hand of God in the events of this period (xxxix. 2–5, 21). The temptation to which Joseph is subjected is a very natural one, especially if Potiphar was, according to the strict meaning of the Hebrew word, a eunuch (Authorized Version "officer"). Joseph's conduct shows him to be a very different man from Reuben and Judah, of whose incontinence mention has been made; and his conduct is determined by his deeply religious nature (verse 9). Yet his present reward is disgrace and unmerited suffering. Nothing is harder to bear than injustice, to suffer for righteousness' sake (1 Pet. ii. 19 f.). Since the "captain of the guard" of xl. 3 f. is apparently Potiphar (xxxix. 1), we may probably infer that he doubted his wife's story from the first, and was later convinced of its falsity. At any rate, by putting Joseph in charge of important prisoners of state, he showed that he considered him dependable. Yet he kept him a prisoner!

Joseph has had already two dreams which needed no interpretation, which were to be gloriously fulfilled; but the premature and probably boastful disclosure of them had thus far had only tragic results for himself. He now shows that he can interpret the dreams of others. Yet with sincere and reverent humility he gives the glory to God. Having interpreted the dreams of these state prisoners, he appeals for the help of the chief butler. It seems remarkable that he should ask him to intercede with Pharaoh on behalf of one who is a mere slave, instead of simply asking for his good offices, if restored to power, with his master Potiphar. But Joseph has a God-given sense of destiny which enables him to meet trials, temptations, and vexing delay without losing heart.

"For indeed I was stolen away" (verse 15). Joseph cannot bear to reveal the shameful story of his "selling" into slavery. "Land of the Hebrews." Joseph was known in his master's household as a Hebrew (cf. "Abram the Hebrew", xiv. 13). Except in these chapters and in Exodus i–x, this name is used rarely in the Bible. It seems to have some connection with *Eber* (x. 21) and also with the expression "beyond (*eber*) the river", which may be used both with reference to the Euphrates and the Jordan. Its connection with the word *Habiru* which occurs in Babylonian (e.g. in the Amarna Letters) and with *'Apiru* which occurs in Egyptian records, is not clear. These latter words may be broader in scope and yet be applicable to the Hebrews. Joseph's use of the expression suggests family pride, and perhaps familiarity on his part with the splendid prospects of his race as foretold in the Abrahamic covenant.

Pharaoh is not a personal name, but a title meaning "great house" (cf. *Sublime Porte*, as used of the Sultan of Turkey). Consequently, we cannot be sure which Pharaoh is referred to. It is probable that he was one of the Hyksos kings, and since the Hyksos were Semitic invaders, this would account in part for the favour he showed to Joseph's family. If the Exodus took place *circa* 1450 B.C. and the sojourn in Egypt began in 1665 B.C., this event would fall within the Hyksos period.[1]

The failure of the writer to name the Pharaoh may be explained in several ways. The simplest is that his main concern is with God's dealings with Israel. He is interested in Egypt only indirectly. Consequently, he has little to say about matters which to the secular historian would be of great interest and importance. The fact that he mentions the names of Joseph's master, Joseph's wife, and of the two midwives, justifies the conclusion that he knew and could have given the names of the Pharaohs who figure in his narrative. The assertion has been made that he did not mention them because he did not know them, and the inference is drawn that the narrative must have been written centuries

[1] The length of this period has been much debated. Josephus made it 511 years. Petrie's last estimate was about 800 years. Other scholars reduce it very greatly, to 200 years or even 150 years. Even the lowest estimate would permit the identifying of the Pharaoh of Joseph's time with a Hyksos monarch. This makes the references to "Egyptians" significant (xxxix. 1, 2, 5, xliii. 32, xlvi. 34).

after the time of Moses. Both assertion and inference are
alike gratuitous.

After long delay—two full years—which must have sorely
tested his faith in his fellowmen and in his God, Joseph's
opportunity arrives. Pharaoh dreams; and there is no one to
interpret. The chief butler recalls his prison experience. "I
do remember my faults this day" (verse 9), he says. Yet
he recalls only his own misfortune, and makes no mention
of his sin of ingratitude towards Joseph (xl. 23). It is only
the thought that Joseph may be of use, which recalls the
Hebrew to his mind. "And they brought him hastily" is in
the Hebrew "caused him to run" (verse 14). Pharaoh must
not be kept waiting by a Hebrew slave. The mention of
shaving is one of those incidental touches which prove the
story to be true to the life of the times. It is noteworthy that
the writer first records the dreams as dreamed by Pharaoh,
and then has Pharaoh relate them to Joseph. Such repetition
is not unusual in the Bible. It is often clearly for emphasis.
Cf., for example, Genesis xxiv; Numbers vii.

"The dream of Pharaoh is one" (verse 25). This is obviously
true, and in their general features both seem quite simple.
Yet these dreams, like the New Testament parables, are
intended both to reveal and conceal truth. And Joseph, as
did Daniel under similar circumstances, ascribes to God his
ability to interpret them.

"And for that the dream was doubled" (verse 32). We
wonder whether, as he predicts the certain and prompt fulfilment of the dream, Joseph is reminded that his own dream
was doubled (xxxvii) and draws from this the comforting
assurance that his own troubles are nearly at an end. It
seems almost too much to imagine, yet probably we are
intended to infer that in his picture of the indispensable
man (verse 33), and especially in the programme which he
proposes for him to follow, Joseph is suggesting himself. Yet
Pharaoh at once recognizes his fitness, and the humble slave
becomes the all-powerful vizier.

Few men, if any, have been raised to prominence and power
as suddenly as was Joseph. His investiture with authority
must have been very imposing. But it is briefly described, as
are also the steps which he took to put into effect the advice
he had given Pharaoh. "One-fifth", during years of unparalleled

plenty, does not seem at all excessive, and if the reason for such a levy was made public the people would be encouraged also to save for themselves. Verses 48 f. suggest that Joseph did not confine himself merely to collecting the one-fifth levy, but bought all that he could lay his hands on in addition. That he stored up plentiful reserves appears from verse 57. For otherwise he would not have been in a position to sell to foreigners. The mention of "all countries" as coming to buy grain prepares us for the resumption of the personal and family history of Jacob's sons. Except for xlvii. 13–26, the broader aspects of the story are practically ignored. The writer is not giving us a history of Egypt, but of Jacob and his family in Egypt.

The bringing of Jacob to Egypt is to be the climax of the narrative. The way it was brought about makes a story of intense human interest. That four chapters should be devoted to what we might call preliminaries and dismiss as unnecessary details, shows how important the inspired writer considered them to be. Two journeys are required to accomplish the result. Joseph's treatment of his brothers shows shrewdness and common sense, although he uses methods which we cannot fully justify, but can easily, perhaps too easily, condone when we consider the unlimited power at his disposal and the provocation he had received. His deep love for his kindred, especially Jacob and Benjamin, appears again and again. Yet why, for nine years, with all the resources of Egypt at his disposal, he made no effort to secure an answer to the question of xliii. 27 and xlv. 3, we are not told.

Joseph's love for Benjamin is intense. Yet he does not hesitate to charge him with theft and claim him as a slave. He accuses his brothers of lying and yet is himself guilty of trickery and deceit. His intentions are good. His determination to test his brethren is eminently proper. His loving and forgiving spirit, his constancy in adversity, his self-restraint when raised to power, his consciousness of divine guidance— all of these things taken together make Joseph a wonderfully attractive and beautiful character. Yet he is not perfect. The Bible tells us of the sins and failures of its heroes, lest we be hero-worshippers.

As in the case of Abraham, the story is told only as it concerns the principal characters. The narrative suggests that there were ten men, ten sacks, ten asses. But this is probably due solely to the brevity and simplicity of the story. Genesis xi. 31 mentions only four persons. Yet Abraham had very many men-servants and women-servants. He had flocks and herds and herdsmen. The trained men born in his house numbered 318. Jacob had returned from Mesopotamia with much cattle, etc., and Jacob's sons describe themselves as shepherds and herdsmen. Ten ass-loads of grain would not have sufficed for long for a household numbering some hundreds of souls. So we may assume that the ten brethren are mentioned as the chief and responsible persons, and their servants, whether many or few, are disregarded.

Joseph cannot have supervised personally and in every detail the sale of grain to the Egyptians and to all foreigners. But as a good administrator, he kept in touch with everything. He may have required that in the case of foreigners their nationality be carefully inquired into and reported to him, especially if the caravan was a large one and wanted to buy much grain. At any rate the case of these Hebrews was reported to him, and he took personal control. He at once recognizes them, and sees God's hand at work; but he is naturally suspicious and decides to test their sincerity. He accuses them of being spies. This charge may mean that at this time the Egyptians regarded foreigners with more than ordinary suspicion, since their own abundant resources in a time of famine might lead their enemies to attack and plunder them. Such a fear was only natural, since Asiatic nomads had often made incursions across the frontier.

In their answer, which apparently implies that a father would not risk *ten* sons on a dangerous mission (as spies) which one or two might accomplish equally well, they disclose facts of which Joseph at once takes advantage. They are to be regarded as guilty until they prove their statements. One of them shall go for Benjamin, while the others are kept in prison. This high-handed decree of the autocrat is then modified, with a show of generosity and piety which does not make it any less arbitrary: one shall remain, Simeon, the others shall go for Benjamin. Autocratic! Yet Joseph weeps, and apparently as slight amends returns their money to them, a gesture which is a cause of anxious surmisings: "they were afraid". And Jacob's summing up is "all these things are against me" (xlii. 36). When the question of taking Benjamin to Egypt to secure the release of Simeon is broached, and Jacob laments and refuses to consider it, Reuben shows his impulsiveness and irresponsibility by a savage proposal: "slay my two sons". No wonder Jacob hesitates to trust them with Benjamin.

The Second Journey (xliii–xlv) makes a still more amazing story. The famine makes it unavoidable (xliii. 1–15). Jacob is forced to yield. The brothers take Benjamin and return to Egypt, with their father's reproaches and laments ringing in their ears, and troubled about the money that has been returned. The reception which they receive amazes them (verses 16–34). Joseph's steward quiets their fears and restores Simeon to them. Their timid excuses are brushed aside as needless, and they are to feast at the viceroy's table. He is graciousness itself. He accepts their gifts, shows Benjamin special honour, and sends them away with lavish supplies and with their money refunded. All seems to be well. Then the blow falls (xliv. 4–13). Benjamin is accused of theft and claimed as a slave! Their cup of woe seems full to overflowing. But Judah's noble appeal leads Joseph to reveal himself, and sorrow is turned into joy (verses 14–34). The story is told with wonderful vividness, in all its human interest, pathos, tragedy, yet with that striking combination of brevity and elaboration (Judah's speech is seventeen verses long) which is so characteristic of the Bible.

The divine providence which is taking Jacob to Egypt is stressed in the vision of xlvi. 1–4. Joseph has already realized it (xlv. 7 f.) and pointed it out to his brothers. But Jacob is given special assurance, perhaps because of xv. 13. Hence the reassuring "Fear not". Nowhere in Scripture is Jacob's going down to Egypt represented as sinful or as showing lack of faith. God has wonderfully prepared the way by making Joseph the governor of that land; and God promises to go with Jacob, and also to restore him to the land of his fathers.

The sojourn in Egypt was not a punishment for sin. It was a period of trial and testing for Israel; and the words, "for there I will make of thee a great nation", suggest that for reasons which we cannot fully understand the change from a shepherd clan to a mighty nation could be better effected in Egypt than in Canaan. In these respects the Egyptian bondage stands in marked contrast to the Babylonian captivity, which was the punishment for incorrigible disobedience (Jer. xviii. 8–10). Yet even in that case it was the best of the people that were first carried into captivity "for their good".

The list given in verses 8–27 names sixty-eight men, including Jacob, and two women. Since Jacob had daughters as well as sons, and his sons had wives and their sons likewise, it is obvious that the words "all the souls" (verse 27) are to be interpreted in terms of the character of the list just given. The different total given in Acts vii. 14 (seventy-five) is due to the inclusion in the LXX version of grandsons of Joseph. Jacob's daughters are menioned several times (xxxiv. 9, xxxvii. 35, xlvi. 7). He had servants (xxx. 43, xxxii. 16) as his father Isaac had (xxvi. 19). Probably, like Abraham's 318 servants, most or all of them were "born in his house" and had received the covenant sign (xvii. 27). If, as we may assume to have been the case, these servants and their families went with Jacob to Egypt (xlvi. 32), the caravan may have numbered 1,000 souls, perhaps considerably more. This should be borne in mind in estimating the increase of the Israelites in Egypt.

The manner in which Joseph informs Pharaoh of the coming of his father, and secures Goshen for his brethren, illustrates Joseph's tact and statesmanship, and the reverent homage due to Pharaoh. The dignity of Pharaoh requires that he inform Joseph of his father's arrival, despite the fact that he has learned of it from Joseph. "An hundred and thirty years" (xlvii. 9). Important for the relative chronology. Joseph was thirty-nine when his father was 130 (xli. 46, 53, xlv. 11, xlvii. 28).

The family history of Israel, which is the main interest of the historian, is here interrupted (xlvii. 13–26) to state how Joseph made use of the famine situation to increase the power of Pharaoh, whose interests he naturally had at heart. But this is told very briefly. It is not of primary importance to this story of Jacob's sons. It should be noted that the archaeologists have discovered that about this time a remarkable change, such as is described here, took place in the economic life of Egypt. This is a welcome confirmation of the Biblical story!

In these chapters (xlvii. 27–xlix. 33) which show us Jacob at his best, the patriarch assumes the rôle of his father Isaac, though in a different way and under very different circumstances, and passes on the blessings of the Abrahamic covenant to his sons who are to be the ancestors of the Twelve Tribes of Israel. The phenomenal increase of the Israelites began during the latter days of Jacob (xlvii. 27). Three important matters are mentioned: Jacob exacts a promise from Joseph (xlvii. 29 f.) that he will bury him with his fathers in Machpelah, and he also commands all his sons to the same effect (xlix. 29 f.); Jacob raises his grandsons Ephraim and Manasseh to the rank of sons, thus giving the birthright, a double portion (Deut. xxi. 17), to Joseph (1 Chron. v. 1 f.); and he exalts Ephraim over Manasseh (xlviii).

The blessings pronounced by Jacob (xlix) are expressed in rather enigmatic language, which in some cases involves a word-play on the name of the patriarch. For instance, Judah means "praise", Dan means "judge", Gad may mean "troop" or "fortune" (verse 19 uses the former). The curses pronounced on Simeon and Levi are especially noteworthy, because Levi's is fulfilled in terms of blessing. Because of obedience at a later crisis in Israel's history (Exod. xxxii. 28), Levi was set apart to the service of God (Deut. xxxiii. 8-11) and its scattering among the tribes became a distinction and honour. In a similar crisis, Simeon was apparently a leader in apostasy (Num. xxv). The tribe lost heavily during the years of wandering, and later almost disappeared from the record.

The pre-eminence of Judah is definitely announced (verses 8-12); and the metaphor of the lion's whelp suggests that this will be due to martial prowess, while the figure of the vine suggests the fertility of his land and the wealth and prosperity of his people.

The interpretation of the Shiloh prophecy (verse 10) is difficult. The language is ambiguous, as is sometimes the case in prophecy. "Until Shiloh come" or "until he come to Shiloh" are equally possible renderings. The word "Shiloh" is regarded by some as an epithet "the peaceable one"; others take it as a compound word meaning "he whose it is (come)" or "(he comes to) what is his" (cf. Ezek. xxi. 27). Commentaries should be consulted. The prophecy is certainly Messianic in that it gives the pre-eminence among the tribes to Judah. Whether the person of the Messiah is here introduced is less certain. It should be remembered that this verse is not quoted in the

New Testament, and the name Shiloh nowhere appears as a
title of the Messiah, unless it is implied in the title "Prince of
peace" (Isa. ix. 6).

Joseph's blessing is even longer than Judah's. The birthright
of the first son of Leah passed to Joseph, the first son of
Rachel, and found expression in the "double portion" given
to Joseph by the raising of his two sons to the status of *sons*
of Jacob, and therefore to headship of tribes. Joseph's own
merit and achievements are given as a reason for this, as well
as the sin of Reuben and the cruelty of Simeon and Levi.
The last clause of verse 24 is difficult. Probably "shepherd"
and "stone" both refer to God, who is "the Mighty One of
Jacob" (cf. Isa. i. 24, xlix. 26) and also Israel's "Rock" (Deut.
xxxii. 4, 15, 18). But the passage is obscure and caution should
be exercised in our use of it. It has been claimed as a support
of the British-Israel theory, according to which this stone is
the one on which Jacob rested his head at Bethel, it was
carried by Jacob to Egypt and entrusted to Joseph, accompanied the Israelites on their journeyings from Egypt to
Canaan, was the "rock" which Moses smote at Rephidim and
Kadesh, was the "pillar" on or by which the kings of Israel
were crowned, was carried to Ireland after the destruction of
Jerusalem by Nebuchadnezzar, became the coronation stone
of Tara and then of Scone, and is now in the Coronation Chair
in Westminster Abbey. This theory has been supported by
the most extravagant claims.[1] The Bible student should be
careful to distinguish between the possible, the probable, and
the certain. He should also remember that he is required
neither to add to nor to take away from what is contained in
Holy Writ.

[1] It is hard to see how a cautious and careful student of the Bible and
of secular history can see in the thirteen American Colonies a proof that
America is Manasseh, the thirteenth tribe, and in the number thirteen
a reference to the Revolutionary War (Gen. xiv. 4). Twelve was the
number of the tribes from the beginning (Gen. xxxv. 22) and it will be
so at the end (Rev. xxi. 12). The raising of Ephraim and Manasseh to
tribal status was offset by the taking of the tribe of Levi for the special
service of the sanctuary. The Levites were taken in place of the first-
born of all the tribes (Num. iii. 45). This made them the representatives of all Israel at the sanctuary. They ceased to constitute a tribe in
the sense that other sons of Jacob were tribes, and are usually called
"sons of Levi" or "Levites". The Bible never speaks of thirteen tribes
or of Manasseh as the thirteenth.

Jacob's burial (l. 1–14) is described rather fully to show the honour in which Joseph was held by Pharaoh and the Egyptians. How unable Joseph's brethren were to appreciate the nobility of Joseph's character is shown by the incident in l. 15–21.

The extreme brevity with which the story is now brought to a close, for Joseph is still in his prime and has more than fifty years to live, may simply mean that all has been said that needs to be said. Perhaps it suggests that Joseph's public career was nearly ended, and that the last years of his life were uneventful. A change of rulers may have deprived him of his exalted position. As to this we can only surmise. What we are told is that Joseph died in confident hope of the fulfilment of the promise to the fathers. But he does not ask to be buried at once in Machpelah, with the honours which he and the Egyptians had rendered his father Jacob. His body is to remain in Egypt until the time of restoration arrives. Then it is to return in the midst of those who return to the land of promise (Exod. xiii. 19). So Joseph's bones are placed in a coffin in Egypt. No eulogy is pronounced upon Joseph. His life is a sufficient eulogy!

EXODUS

As the last of the "generations" in Genesis is mainly concerned to make clear that the "going down" of Jacob
and his sons into Egypt was *of God,* so nearly half of
Exodus has as its great theme the thrilling story of how God
delivered Jacob's descendants from Egyptian bondage and
made them His peculiar people, in fulfilment of His promise
to Abraham, His friend (Gen. xv. 14, xlvi. 4, l. 24; Exod. ii. 24,
iii. 8, 10, 16, vi. 1–9). The long years of the sojourn are scarcely
more than mentioned.

The Book of Exodus[1] has three main divisions: Israel in
Egypt (i. 1–xii. 36), the journey to Sinai (xii. 37–xix. 2), Israel
at Sinai (xix. 3–xl. 38). It describes the call of Moses, the
conflict with Pharaoh, the crossing of the Red Sea, the giving
of the Law, and the making and erecting of the tabernacle,
events of the greatest importance in the history of the people
of God.

I.—Israel in Egypt (i. 1–xii. 36). "Now (or, and) these are the
names" (i. 1–5). The long genealogy of Genesis xlvi. 8–27 is
summarized in terms of Jacob and his twelve sons. But the
total "seventy souls" is repeated. Thus it is made perfectly
clear that *all* of Jacob's sons were in Egypt. This is important
since it is claimed by many of the critics that only the
"Joseph" tribes were in Egypt. This theory finds no support
in the Bible and is flatly contradicted by such statements as
this one with which Exodus begins. That the historian should
begin his account of the deliverance from Egypt in this way
shows how important he regarded this fact to be, that all the
descendants of Jacob experienced the wonderful events which
he now proceeds to describe. This brief and summary introduction concludes with the statement: "And the children of
Israel were fruitful, and increased abundantly, and waxed

---

[1] The name "Exodus" is taken over from the Greek Version. It is an
appropriate name except for the fact that it is not sufficiently comprehensive. The Jews call it *Shemoth* (Names), or *We'elleh Shemoth*
(and these are the names).

exceeding mighty; and the land was filled with them" (verse 7). Clearly, the writer does not find difficulty with the phenomenal increase of the children of Israel. He glories in it.

The Rise of an Oppressor is recounted in i. 8–22. The reference to a new king who knew not Joseph may point to a change of dynasty, such as occurred with the expulsion of the Hyksos by Ahmosis, the first king of the XVIII Dynasty about 1580 B.C. This would give a double reason for oppressing the Hebrews: the fact that they were Semites, and the phenomenal increase of these foreigners in Egypt. These repressive measures, as always happens, steadily increased in severity (verses 9–22). The mention of the land of Rameses (verse 11) need not mean that Rameses II was the Pharaoh of the oppression.[1] In Genesis xlvii. 11 we read that Joseph settled his family in the land of Rameses. (In the Hebrew both words are spelled the same way.) The mention of two Hebrew midwives (verse 15) may mean only that they were the principal and responsible ones. Note also the reason they give to Pharaoh: usually their services were not needed. The names of the midwives are recorded. The names of Pharaoh and of Pharaoh's daughter are not. No reason is given, but the fact is significant of God's estimate of values.

The account of the Raising up of the Deliverer (ii) is an instructive example of Hebrew narrative prose. It is told with great simplicity and modesty: "a man of the house of Levi" married "a daughter of Levi", "And the woman conceived, and bare a son". In this way, the all-important event, Moses' birth, is introduced as briefly as possible. Other relevant facts are mentioned only when and as needed; that he had a much older sister (verse 4), named Miriam (xv. 20 f.), and a brother named Aaron (iv. 14), who was three years his senior (vii. 7). The first four statements of chapter ii cover, or we may say ignore, a period of a dozen years or more, in order to plunge us at once *in medias res*.

That Pharaoh's daughter (verses 5–10) was the famous

[1]The view that Rameses II was the Pharaoh of the Oppression was proposed by Bunsen and Lepsius, and gained many adherents. It is beset with the great difficulty, not to mention others, that the 480 years of 1 Kings vi place the Exodus about 1450 B.C. or nearly two centuries earlier than this monarch. Thothmes III was, like Rameses, a great conqueror and builder; and he may well have been the Pharaoh who "knew not Joseph" and oppressed the children of Israel.

Hatshepsut, kinswoman and queen of Thothmes III, is a very attractive supposition. That Moses was not only saved from death but made the "son of Pharaoh's daughter" shows, as was said of Joseph, that *God was with him.* There is even a touch of humour in the paying of Moses' mother to nurse her own son. God makes even the wrath of men to praise Him. The life of Moses divides naturally into three periods of forty years each.

The *First Period* of Moses' life is described very briefly (ii. 1–15), most of it being summed up in the words, "when Moses was grown". Acts vii. 22 states that he "was instructed in all the wisdom of the Egyptians, and he was mighty in his words and works.[1] At the age of forty, Moses makes a high-handed and futile attempt to help his people. His slaying of the Egyptian shows him to be a man of powerful emotions which he does not always succeed in controlling (Num. xx). The New Testament stresses two points, Moses' love for Israel and belief in their destiny (Heb. xi. 25 f.), and his confidence in their responsiveness (Acts vii. 25). The one was amply rewarded, the other met with constant disappointment.

The *Second Period* of forty years (ii. 16–iv. 17), like the first, is given only in barest outline except for the momentous incidents with which it closes. It was the sufferings of Israel in Egypt (ii. 23–5) which led to the call of Moses. Otherwise Moses would have lived out his life in Midian as the son-in-law of Jethro. But the God of their fathers, the God who had made a covenant with Abraham, Isaac, and Jacob, remembered His promise and called Moses to be the deliverer of His people. This deliverance is repeatedly described (iii. 10, 12, vi. 4, 8, xiii. 5) as the fulfilment of God's promise to the fathers (Gen. xii. 1–9, etc., xlvi. 4).

Those who are unwilling to believe that Abraham was a monotheist (Gen. xxiv. 3) and that it was the God of Abraham, Isaac, and Jacob, who appeared to Moses at the bush, are disposed to derive the religion of Israel from the religions of the neighbouring peoples, and to attribute the transformation of crude and immoral polytheism into a lofty ethical mono-theism to the "genius of the Jew for religion", especially as shown in the teachings of the great prophets of the eighth

---

[1] Josephus' account of the birth of Moses and of his career in Egypt stands in sharp contrast to the sober one given in the Bible.

and seventh centuries B.C. A favourite theory with them is the so-called Kenite theory. Briefly stated, it is that Jethro the priest of Midian was a Kenite, that the Kenites were metal workers (smiths), worshippers of the God of the fiery mountain (a volcano), that Moses received and adopted this worship while in Midian, and at the "Mount of God" pledged the Israelites to the worship of this fire god, the god of Sinai, who finally transferred his habitat to the land of Canaan. Such a theory is utterly out of harmony with the Biblical record. It was the God of his *fathers* who appeared to Moses.

The genius of Israel throughout the centuries was for apostasy. They did not rise gradually from polytheism to monotheism. They fell back repeatedly from monotheism to polytheism. The constant appeal of the prophets was that they return to the *God of their fathers.*

The Call of Moses (iii–iv) is one of the great moments in human history. It is told so simply that a child can understand it. Yet it is awe-inspiring. It suggests Solomon's question (1 Kings viii. 27). Here we see the God whose voice was to shake the earth at Sinai (Exod. xix; Heb. xii. 26), talking, arguing, pleading even, with a mere man to undertake a great work. And who is this man? One of the conspicuous failures of history. Born of a slave people, raised to high position, well educated, capable of great things, Moses had slain an Egyptian for smiting a Hebrew, he had tried to make peace between two Hebrews. With what result? Career ruined, flight, exile, an unknown and forgotten man for forty years— forty years to repent of having assumed the rôle of deliverer. And suddenly to this failure of a man comes the call of God to deliver his entire people. The man who has failed in a small way is summoned to undertake in a large way! God's ways are not our ways!

Fire is often a sign of the presence of Deity (Exod. xix. 18 f.; Deut. iv. 24; 1 Kings xviii. 38). The marvel is not that the bush burns, but that it does not burn up, "is not consumed". Moses is curious and turns aside. Then God speaks: first a word of warning, then of explanation, then a summons to service. It is significant that "the angel of the Lord" (verse 2) is called "God" in verse 3 and "God" and "Lord" in verse 4. Cf. xxiii. 20 where it is said of the Angel of the covenant, or the Angel of the Lord, "my name is in him", which is equivalent to "I am in him". This indicates that this pre-eminent Angel is the pre-incarnate Christ. When Moses hesitates to accept the call of God, he is given a "token" or sign which is strikingly different from those which he receives for the people and for Pharaoh. It is a challenge to his faith in God and his love for his people (verse 12); and this summons to do the seemingly impossible is wonderfully confirmed at Sinai, when Moses returns (iii. 1, xix. 2) to the mount with the people and they worship the God of their fathers.

Moses is told God's name (iii. 13 f.): "I am" represents the first person (*ehyeh*) of the imperfect of the verb "to be", of which the name *Lord*, i.e. Jehovah (*yahweh*)[1] would then be the third person, and mean "He is" or "He will be". It would then describe God either as the One who *is*, the self-existent and eternal, or as the One who reveals Himself ("I will be what I will be") in word and deed. That this name was not unknown to Moses is clearly indicated (verse 15). Moses is given signs for Israel and for Pharaoh. He is also given Aaron as a "prophet", or spokesman. For a prophet is one who speaks the words put in his mouth by another (iv. 14–16).

Moses secures Jethro's consent apparently without taking him into his confidence. Why he takes his family with him to Egypt (iv. 18–28) and why he later sent them back (xviii. 2) we do not know. The words of verse 19 suggest that Moses did not act as promptly as he should have done. There was

[1] In Hebrew the Memorial Name (Exod. iii. 15) is written JHWH. Hence it is often called the Tetragram (i.e. four-letter word). In later times the Jews hesitated to pronounce it, and in reading the Old Testament substituted for it the word "Lord" (*Adonay*); and when the "vowel-points" were added to the consonantal text they placed the vowels of the word "Lord" with the consonants of the Tetragram, in order to indicate that "Lord" was to be substituted for it in reading. At the time of the Reformation, when the study of Hebrew was revived, it was mistakenly supposed that these vowels were really the vowels of the Tetragram; and this resulted in the pronunciation "Jehovah". But the LXX uses the word "Lord"; and the New Testament does the same (cf. Ps. cx. 1; Matt xxii. 44) The Authorized Version follows this New Testament usage in most cases (printing the word as LORD) and the word LORD is retained in the E.R.V. The use of "Jehovah" in A.R.V. is unfortunate, for the double reason that it is not the correct pronunciation of the Tetragram and that it insists in retaining in the Old Testament a name which never appears in the New Testament, and rejecting a substitute which has the *approval* and *authority* of the New Testament.

only one "rod of God", though it was sometimes used by Aaron and even called his rod. The rod mentioned in Numbers xvii is, of course, quite different. "My son" (cf. Gen. xii. 30), "my first born". Here the word "son" is used of the nation. But the command to "love" God (Deut. vi. 5) is personal and individual. Verses 24–6 indicate that Moses as a father had neglected to observe the rite of circumcision, a serious offence (Gen. xvii. 14; cf. Joshua v. 5) which had to be expiated before he could enter upon his great vocation. The meeting with Aaron (verses 27 f.) and their conference with the elders of Israel (verses 29–31) prepares the way for the great struggle or duel with Pharaoh.

The conflict with Pharaoh (v. 1–x. 29) is introduced abruptly by the words: "Thus saith the Lord God of Israel, Let my people go." The formula "Thus saith (the Lord)", cf. iv. 22, occurs repeatedly in this narrative. It was clearly a common or usual way of introducing a message (cf. Gen. xlv. 9; Num. xx. 24, xxii. 16; Judges xi. 15; 2 Kings i. 11). Often, as here, it introduces a command. Jehovah throws down the gauntlet to Pharaoh, with the words, "Let my people go", which are only softened by the moderateness of the demand, "that they may hold a feast unto me in the wilderness". Strange words to be uttered in the presence of mighty Pharaoh! "Who is the Lord that I should hearken unto His voice to let Israel go?" Amazement, anger, irritation, sarcasm, we can hear them all in this exclamation, which is followed by emphatic and disdainful refusal: "I know not the Lord, neither will I let Israel go." And the terrors of the ten plagues and the destruction of Pharaoh's army supply the answer. Pharaoh (vii. 17, viii. 10, 22, ix. 14, 29) and the Egyptians (vii. 5, xiv. 4, 18) and also Israel (vi. 7, x. 2, xvi. 6, 12) shall "know" the mighty power of the God of Israel.

It will be recalled that the formula, "Thus saith the Lord", is to become one of the most familiar introductions to the messages of the Prophets, who as men of God spoke as the messengers of God. And the great burden of their message was that Israel and the nations might "know" the Lord.

Pharaoh not only refuses the demand of the Lord; he increases the burdens of the people. No straw will be given them. They try to get stubble to take the place of straw (verse 12). It is not expressly stated that they made bricks without stubble. They naturally blame Moses and Aaron for their evil state. "Now shalt thou see what I will do to Pharaoh" (vi. 1). Pharaoh does not know the Lord at all; and Israel does not know Him enough to trust Him.

"By My name Jehovah was I not known unto them" (vi. 3). The best and simplest explanation of these words is the one indicated by the words we have just been considering, "and they shall know that I am Jehovah". That the *name* Jehovah was known and used long before the time of Moses, is clearly indicated (Gen. iv. 26). But the full redemptive *significance* of the name was not revealed until the exodus. That the name of the God of Israel was Jehovah, was a matter of complete indifference to Pharaoh. To *know* who Jehovah was, that was to become a matter of the utmost concern to him and his people, and of the utmost importance to Israel as well (cf. Exod. xxxiv. 6 f.). The "critics" insist that this verse means that the *name* Jehovah was unknown up to the time of Moses. Hence they argue that the narratives of the Pentateuch are contradictory and must be derived from different sources. This is one of their main arguments in support of the claim that the Pentateuch is composite and not by Moses. Such a view is destructive of the unity and authority of Scripture.

The Ten Plagues which were mighty signs and wonders (vii. 3) contain both a natural and a supernatural element. Frogs, lice, flies, murrain, etc., were all natural phenomena or "pests" well known to the Egyptians. But the record makes it plain that the plagues were far more than mere natural phenomena. They came and went at the command of Moses; they were visited on the Egyptians, not on the Hebrews (cf. esp. xi. 7). They were evidences of the sovereign power of the God of Israel over Pharaoh, the Egyptians, and their gods. Those who are tempted to minimize or rationalize these wonders of old should read carefully Moses' appraisal of them as given in Deuteronomy iv. 34–40.

Pharaoh's reaction to the Lord's demands by Moses is mentioned again and again: (i) his heart "was hardened" (e.g. vii. 13, 22) or "the Lord hardened it" (ix. 12, etc.); (ii) "he hearkened not" (vii. 13, etc.); (iii) "as the Lord had said" (vii. 13, etc.). It is not to be assumed that "was hardened" and "the Lord hardened" are synonymous expressions. In the case of the incorrigibly wicked, the hardening of their hearts is a judicial punishment. God gave Pharaoh both reason and opportunity to yield: when he refused, God hardened him in his evil purpose. The best commentary on this subject is Paul's discussion of it in Romans ix. 8–24, where this conflict is referred to as one of the outstanding illustrations of God's sovereignty in election, in grace, and in judgment. For the Christian the all-important truth is that salvation is of grace, that faith is the gift of God (Eph. ii. 8), and that the Christian must walk in the Spirit lest he be hardened by the deceitfulness of sin.

The Slaying of the First Born (xi. 1–xii. 36) is the last and most terrible of the plagues, and it is treated with especial fullness. The slaying is already referred to in iv. 23, but its announcement to Pharaoh was probably not made until the time for this final display of God's sovereignty had arrived. x. 28–xi. 8 probably describes a single interview, and verses 1–3 are largely parenthetical. Unlike the other plagues, this final act of judgment and deliverance is connected with a special rite or feast, the passover. It is the blood of the pass-over lamb which saves Israel from the Destroyer (xii. 12 f.). Consequently, the account in xii. 2–28 deals both with the original passover and with future observances of the feast as "an ordinance for ever". This is made clear by comparing verses 14–20 with verses 34, 39. The reason for the feast of unleavened bread is stated to be that Israel left Egypt *in haste*. They ate unleavened bread because they had no time to leaven it. It rested on a quite different basis from the prohibition of the use of leaven in the passover and with the sacrifices which were placed on the altar.

xii. 35, "asked" not "borrowed" (Authorized Version). As Pharaoh's daughter paid Moses' mother to nurse him, so the Egyptians paid the Israelites to leave Egypt; and this "spoiling of the Egyptians" may be regarded as "back-pay" for all the slave labour of Israel in Egypt.

II.—The Journey to Mount Sinai (xii. 37–xix. 2). The magnitude of the exodus of Israel from Egypt and all that it involved is pointed out at the very beginning by the statement of the size of the multitude which is to be transported from Egypt to the land of promise.

"About six hundred thousand" (verse 37). This corresponds very closely with the more precise figures given later. It may be based on the "tally-lists" of the overseers, and indicates that the Israelites were organized both in tribes and families, and also in labour gangs. Such an organization made the hasty flight possible. It necessitates an estimated total reaching several millions. This immense total is regarded by many scholars as preposterous; and various attempts have been made to reduce it within "reasonable" bounds. That there are many and obvious difficulties with it cannot be denied. Two things are especially to be noted: (i) The Bible stresses the amazing increase of Israel in Egypt (e.g. i. 7). (ii) It emphasizes the divine aid, guidance, and sustenance which Israel received. When the supernatural factors receive the attention which they deserve, the difficulties largely disappear. That the figure which is given here and more fully elsewhere is correct is indicated very clearly by the totals given for the "silver levy" (xxxviii. 25). The size of the "mixed multitude" (verse 38) which accompanied Israel is not stated. The word is apparently from the same root as the word for "woof". It suggests a heterogenous, interwoven mass. It is referred to in Numbers xi. 4. Probably the blasphemer of Leviticus xxiv. 10 f. belonged to this class. A somewhat similar situation is described in Nehemiah xiii. 3.

xii. 40: "Now the sojourning . . . *was* four hundred and thirty years." This is the so-called "long" chronology for the period of the oppression in Egypt. The Samaritan-Hebrew text of the Pentateuch and the Greek (LXX) version have the additional phrase "in the land of Canaan". Whether this is the original reading or a later addition has been much debated.[1] It is called the "short" chronology, because it divides the 430 years exactly in half, 215 years in Canaan, 215 years in Egypt. The short chronology was adopted by Usher; and it appears in the margins of many editions of the Authorized Version.

Verse 42: "a day much to be observed". The deliverance from Egypt is very frequently referred to in the Old Testament

[1] The problem is a difficult one. In Galatians iii. 17 Paul speaks of the law as coming 430 years after the covenant. This seems to support the short chronology rather definitely. But it seems at least possible that Paul was thinking of the entire sojourn in Canaan in terms of the word "covenant" (Gen. xlvi. 3 f. may be regarded as a final renewal or reaffirmation of it to the patriarchs); and that he did not mean to include it in the 430 years. Commentaries should be consulted.

(about a hundred times) as the great evidence of God's love to Israel and of His claim to their entire devotion (e.g. Jer. ii. 6; Hos. xii. 13).

The claiming of the first born (xiii. 1–16). Having spared the first born of Israel, the Lord claims them as His own. Hence they are to be redeemed (verse 13). Cf. Numbers iii. 12; Deuteronomy xxxiii. 8–11.

"Every first born of man thou shalt redeem" (xiii. 13). This command is to be carefully noted, since it definitely prohibits one of the most abhorrent of all the religious practices of antiquity, infant sacrifice, a custom which appears to have been common among the Canaanites. It should be obvious that this is an expansion of the brief statement in xiii. 2, and that xxii. 29 is to be interpreted in agreement with it. Even in the case of matters as important as this it should not be necessary to repeat the law in full every time. The general statement is always to be interpreted in terms of the more precise and detailed one. Yet we even find the critics, whose reconstruction of the Old Testament is largely dominated by evolution and the study of comparative religion, asserting that xiii. 2 and xxii. 29 represent an early and primitive form of the (Mosaic?) law which required the sacrifice of infants to Jahweh as in the Chemosh-Molech worship of Ammon and Moab.

"Every firstling of an ass" (xiii. 13). Probably the ass is mentioned as representative of all the unclean beasts which were useful and valuable. In Numbers xviii. 15 this requirement is made to include them all.

Verse 17 f: "The way of the Philistines". By causing the people to turn back toward the south, the Lord apparently purposed to "pocket" them between the Bitter Lakes, which may then have formed a part of the Red Sea, and the mountains to the west. This encouraged the Egyptians to pursue by apparently placing the Israelites at their mercy. Thus it prepared the way for the destruction of Pharaoh's army and a mighty deliverance for Israel. The Lord commands them to go forward into a *cul-de-sac*, that He may open up a path of deliverance through the sea!

Here, as in the case of the Plagues, natural phenomena are made use of, "the strong east wind" and perhaps the tide. But God so uses and amplifies these means that a mighty act of deliverance and judgment is accomplished. The destruction of Pharaoh's hosts by the returning waters is quite as marvellous as the opening up of the path through the sea for Israel.

This marvellous deliverance, which is the final and supreme proof that the Lord is "mightier than all gods" is celebrated in the Song of Moses (xv. 1–18), a magnificent pæan of victory in which highly figurative language is used: the wind is described as "the blast of Thy nostrils". The victory is complete. Of the enemy there is not left as much as one (verse 28); and Israel saw God's mighty hand, and rejoiced; and they feared and believed the Lord and His servant Moses.

The mountain-top experience of God's salvation is speedily followed by the ordinary trials of daily life. For Israel, the most serious of these is the lack of water. The problem is solved temporarily by the use of a seemingly very inadequate means. The Lord used the medicinal properties of the "tree" —as He had used the frogs, the murrain, and the strong east wind—to accomplish results far greater than was inherent in them. The lesson intended for us would seem to be that God would have us use to the full all the natural resources at our disposal, and trust Him to supplement them as the occasion may require by His almighty power.

That the Manna (xvi) was "bread from heaven" (John vi. 31) is made especially clear by the significant fact that a double portion was provided on the sixth day and none on the seventh. By this means the people were taught for forty years the meaning of the petition, "Give us this day our daily bread"; and they were also taught to "remember the Sabbath day to keep it holy". No generation, in the entire course of human history, has been so obviously and constantly *fed* by God. Yet this very generation which received such signal evidence of God's daily care apostatized and perished in the wilderness.

The miracle of smiting the rock (xvii. 1–7) is in some respects the counterpart of the giving of the manna, and should be studied in connection with it. Since the supply of manna was both miraculous and continuous for this entire period (Exod. xvi. 35; Joshua v. 12), it would be inconsistent to argue that the supply of water must have been confined to two widely separated places, Horeb and Kadesh. If the need of water was as constant and imperative as of bread, or more so, the supply must have corresponded to the need. For the stream of water miraculously supplied from the rock at Sinai to have followed Israel on their journeys, is no more impossible, humanly speaking, than for the manna to have continued for forty years (Ps. cvii. 35; Isa. xli. 18, xlix. 10).

To what extent natural means may have been used to bring this about, and to what extent it was entirely miraculous, we cannot say. The route followed by Israel was chosen by God, and the digging of channels by the Israelites themselves at Moses' command may have removed some natural obstacles. On the other hand, the statement that at Kadesh near the end of the forty years "there was no water" (Num. xx. 2) for the people indicates that the supply of water may have ceased, or have been interrupted for shorter or longer periods and for various reasons. (Cf. Num. xx. 19; Deut. viii. 15, ix. 21; Ps. lxxviii. 15–20, cv. 41, cxiv. 8.)

Paul, in referring to this subject (1 Cor. x. 4 f.), declares that both the meat and the drink were "spiritual", which means that they were "from heaven" (John vi. 31) and miraculously supplied. When he goes on to say that they "drank of that spiritual rock that followed them" and adds that this "rock was Christ", we must be careful not to read into his words more than he intended. His exact meaning has been much debated. We may be sure that by describing the rock as "spiritual" he is excluding the Jewish tradition that the literal rock at Horeb or a fragment of it rolled after them wherever they journeyed. We may be equally sure that he saw in the manna from heaven and the water from the rock the types of Christ who is the Source of life to His people as well under the old dispensation as under the new.

How much more may be inferred, it is hard to say. Some hold that the statement that the rock followed them refers to the definite Theophany of the pre-incarnate Christ, the Angel of the covenant (Exod. xxxii. 34, xxxiii. 15). In dealing with such passages, the only safe rule—we may call it the golden rule of exegesis—is that given in Deuteronomy iv. 2 and Revelation xxii. 18 f. We must be careful neither to read into a passage meanings which are not clearly there, nor to read out of it meanings that are clearly there. Sometimes the one extreme may be quite as serious as the other. Equally important is it that we endeavour to interpret any given passage in the light of the teachings of the Bible as a whole.

The reason for Amalek's attack is not stated. It must have been particularly ruthless and dastardly, to account for the fearful curse pronounced on them here (cf. 1 Sam. xv). Whether there is any connection between them and the grandson of Esau (Gen. xxxvi. 12) is doubtful. The identity of name does not establish it. (Cf. the Enochs of Gen. iv. 17 and v. 19.) Numbers xxiv. 20 indicates that Amalek was an ancient people; and unless "country of the Amalekites" (Gen. xiv. 7) is used in a proleptic sense, we must infer that there is no connection.

Jethro (xviii) comes to visit Moses, bringing Zipporah and her two sons.[1] Why Moses had sent them back is not stated (cf. iv. 20). Jethro rejoices in Israel's victories, acclaims and worships Jehovah, and gives Moses advice regarding the administration of justice, which Moses accepts. Then he departs to his own land.

III.—ISRAEL AT MOUNT SINAI (xix. 3–xl. 38). The traditional site of the "mount of God" is near the southern end of the Sinaitic peninsula, in that group of lofty mountains, one of which has borne for centuries the name *Jebel Mousa* (Mountain of Moses). The exact location has been much debated. In recent years the theory has been advanced that the site was in Midian. The claim that none of the volcanic mountains in the Peninsula has been active in historic times will not carry weight with any except those who seek a naturalistic interpretation of the tremendous Theophany which took place there. Nor does the fact that Moses was living with Jethro, the priest of Midian, prove that the "mount of God" was in Midian. We read that Moses led the flock of Jethro to the "back side of the desert", which may have been many miles away. The traditional site is still most generally accepted as the correct one.

[1] The explanation of the name Eliezer ("for the God of my father was mine help", verse 4) shows that Moses regarded Jehovah as the God of his ancestors. Jethro acclaims Jehovah as "greater than all gods". But it is perhaps significant that he brings an offering to *Elohim*, not to *Jehovah*. The Kenite theory of the critics (that Jahweh was a Kenite deity, that Jethro was his priest, and that at Sinai he initiated Aaron and the leaders of Israel into his worship) is contradicted by the entire context. Jethro was apparently a polytheist. He was a "priest of Midian"; but he recognized either actually or as a matter of courtesy the pre-eminence of Jehovah, while refusing to worship him exclusively.

Israel reached Sinai in the third month after a journey of at least six weeks, in the course of which they travelled about 200 miles; they stayed there nearly a year (Num. x. 11). Moses' first stay in the Mount was probably brief. He was to remind the people that the God of the Covenant had delivered them from Egypt, and to offer them the status of a unique people—a kingdom of priests and a holy nation—upon condition of obedience (verses 3–6). We note: (i) While the emphasis is naturally on the recent deliverance by virtue of which Jehovah as their divine Deliverer claimed them as His people (xx. 2), this was because of the Abrahamic covenant (ii. 24, iii. 6, vi. 8). The Mosaic covenant rests on the Abrahamic. (ii) The condition, "if ye will obey my voice indeed", is not new. Abraham's faith was constantly tested in the furnace of obedience (Gen. xxii. 18, xxvi. 5).

The claim which is often made that the Abrahamic covenant was unconditional while the Mosaic was conditioned on obedience, finds no support in Scripture. God's first word to Abram was a Command: "Get thee out of thy country . . . unto a land that I will show thee" (Gen. xii. 1). Abram obeyed this command. The performance of the rite of circumcision was made an indispensable condition to covenant blessing (Gen. xvii). Abram performed it at once. The claim that the Abrahamic covenant was "unconditional" has dangerous implications; for it suggests an antithesis between *faith* and *obedience* which is not warranted in Scripture. Paul joins the two together, when he speaks of the "obedience of faith" (Rom. i. 5, xvi. 26). The condition, "if ye will obey my voice", is merely the echo, we may say, of Genesis ii. 16, "and the Lord God commanded the man". The reply of the people, "All that the Lord hath spoken we will do", was the oath of allegiance of a loyal people to its ruler or king. They did not realize all that it involved, nor how unable they were to keep the law of God. Their words may show self-confidence and self-righteousness. But God's requirement has always been perfect obedience (Gen. iii. 11). And the law which so stresses this requirement also contains and unfolds that system of expiation by sacrifice by means of which the penitent sinner may find forgiveness and acceptance with his God.

This wonderful scene at Sinai was the fulfilment of the "sign" given to Moses (iii. 12) and it must have given him great joy and encouragement. How Moses sanctified the people we do not know, if more was involved than the two things which are mentioned, both of which were important: (i) they washed their garments as symbolic of cleansing; (ii) they were to practise continence (verse 15).

The second requirement is especially noteworthy, when we remember how prominently sensuous and orgiastic rites figured in the religions of the peoples with whom Israel had already come into contact, and of those among whom they were soon to dwell. The religion of Israel is not ascetic. Marriage is both normal and lawful. But the Old Testament draws the golden mean between celibacy and sensuality. Especially is this the case with acts of worship, from which the sensual and sexual is rigidly excluded. This is a remarkable evidence that the religion of Israel was of supernatural origin.

"And the Lord came down upon Mount Sinai" (verse 20). The glory of the Lord had already been manifested repeatedly (xvi. 10). But this Theophany surpasses them all. Fire is the special sign of His Presence (iii. 2, xiv. 24, xxiv. 17, xl. 38). The fire is both consuming and refining (Deut. iv. 24; Heb. xii. 29). The holiness of God, and His separation in holiness are especially stressed. He is in the midst of His people, but apart from them. The awful majesty of the scene is referred to repeatedly by Moses (Deut. iv. 5, ix. 10, 15, x. 4, xviii 16).

The Decalogue.

The Decalogue (xx) opens with "And God spake all these words, saying". The scene was both terrifying and unparalleled (Deut. iv. 32, 33). The fact that the Decalogue was uttered by the voice of God Himself, without any intermediary, human or angelic, is a proof of its unique and enduring importance (Matt. iii. 17). This is further stressed by the fact that God Himself wrote the "ten words" on tablets of stone (xxiv. 12, xxxii. 15 f., xxxiv. 1 f.; Deut. x. 2, 4). They were not written on clay tablets, nor on the scroll of a book. The "two tables (tablets) of stone" are repeatedly referred to, and they constitute the "testimony" (Exod. xxxi. 18, xxxii. 15, xl. 20). Hence the ark in which they were placed was "the ark of the testimony", and the tabernacle was "the tabernacle of the testimony". The close connection between law and grace is illustrated symbolically by the fact that the mercy-seat was immediately above the testimony which was placed in the ark (Lev. xvi. 13).

There were *two* tables. How the laws of the Decalogue were divided between them, we are not told. The fact that the first four consist of duties to God, the rest of duties to man, would constitute a logical and impressive division. That the duties to God precede the duties to man is both natural and necessary. It is the only proper order. Only those who love God can truly love their fellow-men. The great defect in much humanitarian and philanthropic work lies in this, that it tends to make a religion of social service: to ignore the first table of the Law and to make a cult of the second. The true philanthropy of the second table derives both incentive and directive from the first.

The First Commandment: "Thou shalt have no other gods before Me." This clearly means that Israel is to worship Jehovah, and Him only (Deut. vi. 4 f.). Does it deny the existence of other gods (monotheism) or merely prohibit their worship (monolatry)? The answer is given in such passages as Genesis i, xxiv. 3; Exodus xx. 11, which describe the God of Israel as the Creator of heaven and earth. The Old Testament writers, of course, recognize that the nations, and often even Israel herself, worshipped "other gods". But again and again they point out how empty, vain, and sinful is such worship. The people gathered at Sinai have just had a wonderful demonstration of the impotence of the gods of Egypt (xii. 12). Moses' estimate of such gods is given quite clearly in Deuteronomy iv. 28. They are "no-gods", they are "vanities" (Deut. xxxii. 21), while Jehovah is the creator of heaven and earth (Deut. iv. 35, 39, vi. 4, x. 14; cf. Exod. xxxi. 17). Yet, on the other hand, the appeal which they make to men is due to the fact that the worship given to these vanities is really offered to "demons", to Satan and his angels (Deut. xxxii. 17; Ps. cvi. 37). This is made especially clear in 1 Corinthians x. 20. The idol is "nothing", but the worship rendered to it is given to "demons" (cf. Eph. vi. 12) and the powers of darkness are very real and terrible (1 Pet. v. 8) as well as subtle (2 Cor. xi. 14).[1] To many, perhaps the vast

---

[1] Milton, in *Paradise Lost*, pictures the gods of the heathen (Molech, Chemosh, Beelzebub) as mighty chieftains among the hosts of Satan.

majority of the people, these gods doubtless seemed very real, and they were at best only monolaters. This is shown by the sin of Baal-peor (Num. xxv. 1–9) when Israel turned aside to the licentious and idolatrous worship of strange gods. 2 Kings xvii. 33, "they feared the Lord and served their own gods", illustrates very clearly what is forbidden in this commandment. But the teaching of the Pentateuch is definitely monotheistic.

The Second Commandment: "Thou shalt not make . . . thou shalt not bow down to." The prohibition of idolatry is most explicit. This is the next to the longest of the commandments. No "likeness" of any visible object is to be made, nor is anything material to be worshipped. The language is very definite. Deuteronomy iv. 15–40 is the best interpretation of it. At Sinai they saw no form or similitude: they heard only the Voice. Therefore all attempts at visible representation of the invisible God are strictly forbidden. But that this does not prohibit every form of artistic representation in connection with the worship of the invisible God is indicated by the fact that the figures of cherubim were placed on the ark and used on the veil and curtain of the holy of holies; and that the golden candlestick was to have flowers and cups like almond-blossoms (xxv. 18, 33).

No commandment of the Decalogue was more frequently or flagrantly violated and disregarded than this one. Jeroboam's calves became a symbol of the apostasy of the Northern Kingdom. The use of images is destructive of true spiritual religion (Isa. xliv. 9–20). All idolatry is condemned by the fact that the idol is the work of men's hands (Hos. viii. 6). To worship the idol is to worship what man has made, and put it in the place of God. But the God of Israel is a "jealous God". He demands exclusive worship. He will not share His rights with any other.

It is this exclusiveness of the religion of the Old Testament and of the New Testament which has made the devout Jew and the true Christian the objects of hatred and persecution in every age. The early Christians would not have been persecuted for worshipping Jesus as God had they not insisted that "they be no gods which are made with hands" (Acts xix. 26). The great error in the study of Comparative Religion to-day lies in the fact that most of its exponents emphasize the resemblances between the religion of the Bible and the ethnic faiths, and ignore or minimize the differences. Yet the resemblances are of minor importance, while the differences are of fundamental and supreme importance.

"Them that love Me." Love and fear are master motives. Fear of punishment alone keeps those who hate God from breaking His Law. Love constrains those who love Him to obey Him; and their sins will be sins of ignorance and of frailty, for which atonement is possible and is provided. The basic demand of the entire Decalogue is obedience. Neither love nor fear is directly commanded, both are appealed to as motives for obedience.

The Third Commandment: The taking of the name of God in vain involves not only the false, but also the irreverent or trifling use of it. It does not prohibit the taking of an oath in a judicial or religious manner (e.g. Num. xxx; Deut. vi. 13; Joshua ix. 19; 1 Kings ii. 23 f.) and the same is true of the New Testament. Study Matthew v. 34 in the light of Romans i. 9; 2 Corinthians xi. 31; Galatians i. 20.

The Fourth Commandment: "Remember the sabbath day." The form of this commandment is unique and striking. "Remember" means more than "keep in mind". It seems clearly to carry us back to Genesis ii. 1–3. God's resting on the seventh day is the reason that man should keep it holy. It seems probable that the observance of the sabbath had been almost forgotten in Egypt, and we find only meagre traces of it in the patriarchal history. But the word "remember" indicates that this is no new command, but one which goes far back into the history of the race. "Six days shalt thou labour." It is the six days of labour which entitle a man to the rest of the seventh. It is because he has been so largely engrossed in the affairs of the world for six days that man needs the rest and worship of the sabbath.

"Thou shalt not do any work." This command is purely negative. But it would be a mistake to infer that the Jewish sabbath was meant to be a day of idleness. Since it had a special divine sanction, it was the Lord's day. In the light of such passages as Deuteronomy iv. 9–14, vi. 7–9, xi. 18–23, xxxi. 19, 30, xxxii. 44, it is obvious that this day would be pre-eminently the time for meditation on, and instruction in, holy and heavenly things, for the people, and especially for their rulers (Joshua i. 8; Deut. xvii. 18 f.).

To the faithful Israelite the sabbath was a "delight" (Isa. lviii. 13). To the ungodly it was weariness and waste of time (Amos viii. 5). And the same is true of the Christian sabbath to-day. Desecration of the Lord's day paves the way to the breaking of every other commandment of the Decalogue. Keeping it holy is one of the best means of promoting holy living. The sabbath was made for man, and it is of vital importance to man. It is noteworthy that this is the longest of all the commandments.

The Fifth Commandment: "Honour thy father and thy mother." This command properly stands first in the second table, duties to man. For in all our social relationships the home is of first importance. The honouring of parents implies first of all the recognition of their God-given authority. The words "and thy mother" indicate the high position of women under the law of Sinai. The parents are to teach and train their children, to pass on to them in all its fullness the precious heritage of truth which God has entrusted to them (see above). The home is the place for instruction, especially in matters of faith and duty. The Old Testament contains many examples of parents who failed to train their children, and of children who failed to obey their parents. Yet this is the "first commandment with promise" (Eph. vi. 2); and the Bible has many examples of faithful parents and obedient children. True piety and true patriotism are nurtured in the true home. The readiness of many parents to shift to the day-school and to the Sunday-school many or most of their duties and responsibilities as parents, and the readiness of such institutions or of the State to assume or even to claim this responsibility, have in them elements of serious danger.

The Sixth Commandment: "Thou shalt not kill." This is the first of three commandments which are brief and entirely unqualified. Consequently, it is important to ascertain the exact meaning and use of the word "kill". The Authorized Version renders ten different Hebrew words by the one word "kill". The word used here occurs about fifty times in the Old Testament, and is more frequently rendered by "murder(er)" or "slay(er)". More than half of its occurrences are in Numbers xxxv; Deuteronomy iv. 41, 42; Joshua xx and xxi, i.e. in passages which refer to the cities of refuge. This makes it quite plain that what is prohibited is *murder*. This interpretation is in harmony with the teaching of the Old Testament as a whole, which requires capital punishment for certain crimes (Gen. ix. 6; Exod. xxi. 12, etc.) and also approves of "lawful" war (e.g. Deut. xx; Judges vi. 16).

While the New Testament places special emphasis on the duty of love, even to our enemies (Matt. v. 44), it does not radically change the Old Testament interpretation of this Commandment. It does not teach that peace between good and evil is possible (Matt. x. 34 f.) And "If magistrates, as we learn from the thirteenth chapter of Romans, are armed with a right or power of life and death over their own citizens, they certainly have the right to declare war in self-defence" (Charles Hodge).

The Seventh Commandment: "Thou shalt not commit adultery." This commandment deals with the greatest menace to the home, unchastity. Strictly interpreted, the word "adultery" means the violation of the exclusive right of the husband to the affection of his wife. Its primary aim is to prevent a married woman from bearing to her husband children that are not his. By implication it forbids "all unchaste thoughts, words and actions". That the mutual love of husband and wife should be made the figure and type of the relation in which God stands to His people (Isa. liv. 5; Hos. ii. 19 f.; cf. Eph. v. 21–33; Rev. xxi. 2) gives us the best possible illustration of the ideal marriage. The prevalence of divorce, the ease with which it can be obtained, is one of the greatest perils of our modern world.

The Eighth Commandment: "Thou shalt not steal." Here we have the clear recognition of the right of private ownership of property. It is directed primarily, of course, against the lawless individual. But it applies also and equally to the "soulless" corporation, the "boss-controlled" labour union, and the "totalitarian" State.

The Ninth Commandment: "Thou shalt not bear false witness." That the Israelites were acquainted with the principles and methods of orderly legal procedure is clear from such passages as Genesis xxiii and Exodus xviii. False witness was severely punished (Deut. xix. 16, 19). In many cases it involved the breaking of the Third Commandment also. By implication it enjoins the speaking of truth at all times, and forbids all falsehood and dishonesty.

The Tenth Commandment: "Thou shalt not covet." This
final command is in a sense a summary of the five that precede
it. For the sin of covetousness may enter into them all, and
lead to the breaking of them all. Perhaps it is for this reason
that so many details are given. Nothing that a man has is
safe from the hand of the covetous, if it be in his power to
secure it. Nothing can wreck the happiness of a man more
effectually than failure to be content with the things that he
has (Heb. xiii. 5). Envy can make a man's choicest possessions
seem mean and contemptible in his eyes, and fill his life with
bitterness. "Thou shalt not covet . . . anything that is thy
neighbour's" is a most impressive conclusion to this part of
the Decalogue.

Looking back over these Commandments, we observe that
while usually expressed in negative terms, they all imply or
involve a positive attitude. In Deuteronomy, which is largely
concerned (v–xxviii) with repeating, expounding, and applying
it, we find "love" repeatedly demanded. The first table of the
Decalogue is summed up in the words of Deuteronomy vi. 5,
and the second in Leviticus xix. 18, 34, i.e. in terms of *love.*

The immediate effect of the stupendous spectacle which
accompanied the proclaiming of the Decalogue was to inspire
the people with fear, which Moses told them was to keep
them from sinning. The word "fear" deserves careful study,
for in the Bible it gravitates between the extremes of abject
terror and holy and reverent love. Moses loved God: yet he
said, "I exceedingly fear and quake". Not a little of our
religious worship to-day is marked by the lack of reverent
awe. We are tempted to be too "familiar" with God. Love,
however ardent, will always be reverential. Jesus called His
disciples "friends" and "brethren". But Peter and Paul called
themselves His "bondservants"; and while the simple name
"Jesus" occurs very frequently in the Gospels and less frequently in Acts, it is quite rare in the rest of the New Testament.

There has been a marked tendency in recent years to
minimize the importance of the Decalogue. To the critics,
of course, who see in it merely a brief code of laws which
reflects the gradual growth of moral and religious ideas and
ideals in Israel, it can have little or no permanent and divine
authority.

According to those, on the other hand, who set the Gospel in sharp contrast with the Law, the Decalogue is not intended for the present Church Age. This is, they tell us, the dispensation of grace; and the Old Testament law is Jewish and concerns the Kingdom and not the Church. But in the history of the Church the Decalogue has always, especially since the Reformation, occupied an important place in Christian education. The great Catechisms of Protestantism, such as Luther's, the Heidelberg, and the Westminster Shorter and Longer Catechisms, have all stressed the Ten Commandments as of permanent and binding validity. They used to be memorized in the home and the Sunday-school; and they were recited in public worship much more frequently than to-day. And because the solemn "Thou shalt not" of the Law of God, with its clear and sharp distinction between right and wrong is so seldom heard, an easy-going system of morals which has few if any blacks and whites but consists largely of the greys of expediency and self-interest, has become popular even among Christians.

Christians need constantly to remind themselves that *love* is not an easy-going substitute for *law,* but the *fulfilling* of the Law (Rom. xiii. 10); and that the Law is needed both as a warning to those who are tempted to sin and as a pattern for those who are striving after righteousness. The sense in which Jesus regarded the Law as "fulfilled" in the Gospel is made appallingly plain in the Sermon on the Mount (e.g. Matt. v. 21 f.); and His summary of the Decalogue in terms of love to God and love to man (Matt. xxii. 37–40) makes it a counsel of perfection for all men, since even the most advanced in spiritual growth cannot hope to keep it perfectly.

The mention of the altar immediately after the proclaiming of the Decalogue is significant. The very rigour of the Law, and the terrifying holiness of the Law-giver, shows the necessity of expiation. Sacrifice may be offered wherever God manifests Himself. But such worship is to be of the simplest character; earth or unhewn stones are to be used, and every thing indecorous or suggestive is to be avoided.

The Book of the Covenant (xxi–xxiii. 19) contains a large number of statutes which Israel is to observe. That they are of less permanent nature than the Decalogue is indicated by the fact that they deal first of all with slavery, i.e. with an institution which was of great importance in ancient times but which is now recognized as contrary to the spirit of the Gospel. Yet is may be noted that even the New Testament does not expressly condemn it, though it teaches principles with which it is incompatible. Cf. Paul's Epistle to Philemon.

The laws in this Code are very varied, dealing first with persons and then with property. Many of them are repeated and elaborated in the subsequent legislation. Some of them deal with matters of which Paul says it is "a shame even to speak"; and the necessity of stating them indicates something of the depravity and hardness of heart which the Law as the symbol of the moral government of God was unable to overcome (Rom. viii. 3). The Code deals also with ceremonial and ritual: the sabbatic year, the annual feasts, first fruits, leaven, blood. It closes with the blessed promise that an Angel shall guide the people and bring them safely to their destination; and also with a solemn warning against all contamination with the peoples of the land which the Lord will destroy before them.

The covenant is then solemnly ratified by sacrifice and the sprinkling of blood (xxiv. 3–8). Then the leaders of Israel go up into the Mount to partake of a solemn feast of communion, like the peace offerings provided for by the Law.

The statement that they "saw" God must be interpreted in the light of the command not to "come nigh" (verses 1 f.) and the explanation given in verse 10, which describes only the glory which constituted as it were His footstool. Moses later reminds the people that they saw no "similitude" (Deut. iv. 12). Only Moses was permitted to do this (Num. xii. 8; cf. Deut. xxxiv. 10). Yet even this must be interpreted in terms of Exodus xxxiii. 18–23 and John i. 18.

The Tabernacle, God's Dwelling-place in Israel.

The God of Israel, who has delivered His people from Egyptian bondage and brought them to the Mount of God, and who has manifested Himself to them, shown them His glory, and given them His Law, will now condescend to dwell in the midst of the people whom He has received into covenant relation with Himself. So He commands them to prepare a sanctuary (Exod. xxv. 8) that He may dwell among them. It is to be made according to the pattern shown to

Moses (verse 9) and of materials supplied by the people. With
a single exception (xxx. 11 f.) these gifts are to be voluntary,
free-will offerings (xxv. 2–7, xxxv. 5–9, 20–9).

The great importance which attaches to the tabernacle is
shown by the extraordinary care with which it is described.
First, the pattern shown to Moses (xxv. 9, 40; cf. Heb. viii. 5)
is described in detail in seven chapters (xxv–xxxi). Then
nearly five chapters (xxxv–xxxix) are devoted to an account of
the execution of the work, and a concluding summary or in-
ventory (xxxix. 33–43). Then in chapter xl detailed instructions are given regarding the setting up of the tabernacle
(verses 1–15), followed by an equally detailed account of the
execution of the commands (verses 16–33). Finally, after it
has been asserted some twenty times that the guiding and
governing principle, "as the Lord commanded Moses", has
been faithfully observed, the tabernacle is accepted and consecrated, the all-enveloping cloud being the sign of the Lord's
entering into possession of His earthly dwelling-place (verse 34).

This involves considerable repetition. For example, the
pattern of the ark is described in xxv. 10–22, the making of
it in xxxvii. 1–9, its inspection and installation by Moses in
xxxix. 35, xl. 3, 20 f. The fact that the so-called higher critics
have been insisting for many years that this tabernacle never
existed, but is simply an "idealizing" of the tent of xxxiii. 7 by
the priests of the exilic period, who pictured it as a kind of
portable Solomonic temple, shows how little regard they have
even for the most explicit statements of Scripture, when these
statements conflict with their theories as to what the course
of the history of Israel must have been.

Instead of following the order given in Exodus, which varies
considerably, it may be helpful to consider the tabernacle
from the standpoint of the purpose it was intended to serve.
It was to be the dwelling-place of the Lord God of Israel.
Dwelling in the midst of His people, He was to be accessible
to them, yet unapproachable in holiness, His worship being
carefully prescribed in terms of an elaborate ritual performed
by a mediating priesthood. The structure was to express both
the glory of God and man's sense of the appropriate and
beautiful. The Israelites knew something of the splendour
of the temples of Egypt and their elaborate worship; and
this dwelling of their God must do honour to Him and show

forth His praise. But it could not be too elaborate and substantial, for it was to be a readily portable structure of practical utility.

The tabernacle, as is fitting, occupies the centre of the Camp (Num. i. 50, ii. 17). The first sign of the holy separation of their God is the fact that the tabernacle is surrounded on three sides by the tents of the Levites (Num. i. 53, iii. 31-7), while Moses and the priests encamp in front of it (iii. 38). Thus its immediate environs are sacred and sacramental. It faces east (Exod. xxvii. 13). It stands in a court enclosed by curtains (xxvii. 9-19). The enclosure is 100 by 50 cubits (a cubit is about 18 inches). The curtains are of fine twined linen, probably bleached white, although "white" is not mentioned in describing them. They hang from pillars of brass (bronze) which have sockets of the same metal. But their hooks, fillets (rings or connecting rods) and decorations are of silver. The entrance is at the centre of the eastern end of the court; and it is made conspicuous by a hanging 20 cubits wide (xxvii. 16) of blue, purple and scarlet linen "wrought with needle-work", which involved dyeing, weaving, and embroidery. It was supported on four pillars of brass. The height of the pillars is not stated. Being intended to ensure privacy, it was sufficiently high to serve this purpose.

Passing behind the entrance-curtain or screen, the worshipper finds himself in the *court*. Immediately before him, between him and the tabernacle, is the brazen (bronze) altar of sacrifice (xxvii. 1-8), signifying that the way of approach to God is by sacrifice: without the shedding of blood there is no remission of sins (Lev. xvii. 11; Heb. ix. 22). This altar is tended by the priests. The layman may slay his offering; but the priest must perform the sacrifice (Lev. i.-vii). It is within this sacred enclosure that the sacrificial meal (peace offerings) is to be eaten by the offerer and his family (Deut. xii. 7, 18). Near the altar and probably back of it, stands the laver or basin for the use of the priests who perform the sacrifices (Exod. xxx. 17-21). It is not for the use of the people.

Directly behind the altar of sacrifice stands the tabernacle, which only the priests are permitted to enter. Since its dimensions are 10 by 30 cubits, it is probable that the entrance was at the exact centre of the court. There would then be 20 cubits on either side and behind it, a beautifully symmetrical arrangement. The tabernacle consists of two parts. There is a wooden structure (the *mishkan* or dwelling), which forms three sides of a rectangle. It is of boards (10 by 1½ cubits), which stand on end and are held together by wooden bars. All the wood is overlaid with gold (xxvi. 15, 29). These boards, forty-eight in number, form the two sides and rear of a room which is 30 cubits long, 10 cubits wide, and 10 cubits high. Each board fastens by means of tenons into two silver sockets.

At the front, instead of the gilded boards, there is a curtain or screen—the outer veil—which is exactly like the hanging at the entrance of the outer court (xxvi. 36 f.). This veil is supported by five pillars of shittim wood overlaid with gold, resting on five sockets of brass, but with hooks of gold. Beyond this veil there is a second, which divides the interior into two rooms, the holy place and the holy of holies (verses 31–3). This veil differs from the other two only in having cherubim embroidered on it, to symbolize the immediate presence of God. The holy of holies is apparently a perfect cube (10 by 10 by 10 cubits) one-half the size of the holy place.[1]

The dwelling (*mishkan*) has no roof, but instead four coverings, which are stretched over it laterally and cover the top, sides, and rear. The inner covering is exactly like the veil which separates the holy place from the holy of holies. We do not know whether it hung down inside or outside the golden walls of the dwelling. Some think it hung down inside (it was only 28 cubits long). Others think it hung outside the boards, and it is even suggested that the boards were not solid but constructed as a framework through which the cherubim would be seen, framed as it were by the boards. As to this, the record tells us nothing.

Above this covering there is one of goat's hair, which is called the "tent" over the "dwelling" (Exod. xxvi. 7, xxxvi. 14), and is two cubits longer. Above this there is a covering made of rams' skins dyed red (the only mention of red); and above it, still another of seal or porpoise (not badger) skins—making four coverings in all. Since the last three of the coverings form the *tent*, it is possible that they may have been supported by a kind of ridge pole resting on pillars, which would

---

[1] This is not stated in Exodus; but in the temple which doubled the dimensions of the tabernacle, the "house" was twice the size of the "oracle" (1 Kings vi. 15 ff.).

give the appearance of a tent. Otherwise the top would have been flat, and not at all tent-like. As to this also, we have no definite information. But it may be significant that the length of the two outer curtains is not stated. They may have been considerably longer than the other two, and have been pegged to the ground at some distance from the dwelling.

The entire front of the dwelling is concealed, as we have seen, by a veil or screen made of varicoloured linen. The fact that the five sockets for its pillars are of brass connects it with the outer court. But its pillars are overlaid with gold, which is distinctive of the sanctuary. Only the priests are permitted to pass behind this veil. They do so in performance of their duties at the tabernacle. When the ministering priests pass behind this curtain they find themselves in the holy place (xxvi. 33). It is lighted by a golden lampstand having seven lamps (xxv. 31–40), which stands on the left side. Its lamps are to be fed with pure olive oil, and they are tended by the priests (Lev. xxiv. 1–4). It burns from evening until morning (Exod. xxvii. 20 f., xxx. 7 f.; 1 Sam. iii. 3). These verses seem to indicate that it did not burn during the day. We do not need to assume that its light was needed to enable the priests to perform their daily duties. Enough light for that purpose may have come through the outer veil. Its principal significance was undoubtedly symbolic, setting forth Israel's "relation to God as the possessor and reflector of the holy light that was in Him" (Fairbairn). Cf. Zechariah iv and Revelation i. 12.

The *Table of Shewbread* (xxv. 23–30) is on the right side. On it are displayed twelve cakes of unleavened bread, and cups probably containing wine or oil.[1] Apparently they are an offering and memorial of the daily food of the people, which is dedicated to God because received from God. The loaves are changed every sabbath, and having been consecrated to a holy use are on their removal eaten by the priests in the holy place (Lev. xxiv. 5–9). The placing of frankincense on the loaves connects the table of shewbread with the altar of incense, and stresses the idea of an offering.

---

[1] In verse 29 (cf. xxxvii. 16) the words "to cover" should be rendered "to pour out" (Revised Version; cf. Num. iv. 7: "cups or jars for the drink offering"). The mention of such libation bowls as among the utensils of the table and the fact that a drink offering was usually

The *Altar of Incense* is the most important of the furnishings of the holy place. This is indicated by the fact that it stands in front of the veil which separates the holy of holies from the holy place. On it, morning and evening when he trims the lamps, the priest[1] places a pot of incense, kindled with live coals taken from the altar of burnt sacrifice, whose sacred fire, kindled by God Himself, is never to be allowed to go out (Lev. vi. 13). This incense which is to burn perpetually before the Lord (Exod. xxx. 7 f.) symbolizes the prayers of God's people (Ps. cxli. 2; Luke i. 10).

The *Holy of Holies* is separated from the holy place only by the veil. But the cherubim on the veil signify the presence of God. Behind this veil none may pass save only the high priest, and he only on one day in the entire year, the day of atonement (Lev. xvi; Heb. ix. 7). In the holy of holies there is only the ark of the covenant, also called the ark of the testimony, because the tables of stone containing the Ten Commandments (xxv. 16) are in it. Above the ark is the mercy-seat, which is of pure gold and has at either end cherubim of gold whose wings overshadow it. This is the earthly throne of the Lord God of Israel, who "sitteth above the cherubim" (cf. 1 Sam. iv. 4; 2 Sam. vi. 2; Jer. iii. 16). And it is from here, as coming from One who sits enthroned above the ark, that Moses hears the voice of God speaking to him from behind the veil (Exod. xxv. 22; Num. vii. 89), a unique honour not shared by Aaron or any of Aaron's successors in the priesthood.

The holy of holies is in complete darkness, so far as natural light is concerned (1 Kings viii. 12). But it is filled with the brightness of the Shekinah, that light of God's presence, which

---

connected with the meal offering makes it very probable that such the case. If so, the fact that only the shewbread (bread of the presence) is specifically mentioned, is significant.

[1] "And Aaron shall burn" (Exod. xxx. 7 f.). Probably Aaron is to be regarded as representing the priests; we know that in later times the Law was so understood (1 Chron. vi. 49; 2 Chron. xiii. 11, xxvi. 18; Luke i. 5, 9). In the case of the sedition of Korah (Num. xvi) the question at issue is whether the burning of incense before the Lord is a special and distinctive duty and right of the priests (verses 17 f.). The 250 Levites of the company of Korah were seeking to be recognized as priests (verse 10). Consequently we may assume that the burning of incense was a duty of all the priests, and not of the high priest alone.

is seen in the pillar of cloud and of fire, which abides on the tabernacle while Israel rest in their tents, and when it is moved, guides the people on their journey. This cloud denotes the presence of Jehovah (Exod. xxxiii. 14f.) and from this cloud, which has the appearance of fire by night (xl. 38), fire comes forth to kindle the sacred fire on the altar (Lev. ix. 24) which fire is never to go out (Lev. vi. 13), and also to punish the wicked and disobedient (Lev. x. 2; Num. xi. 1–3). It was in fire that the Lord appeared to Moses at the Bush (Exod. iii. 2), in fire that He appeared at Sinai (xix. 18). This manifestation in fire is apparently the "glory" of the Lord (xvi. 7, 10, xxiv. 16 f.; Num. xiv. 10, xx. 6). It was such a glorious vision of God which the Seventy "saw" in the Mount (Exod. xxiv. 10). It is interesting to compare Isaiah xxxi. 9, xxxiii. 14 in the light of Deuteronomy iv. 24. It is also to be noted that Jerusalem is called Ariel by Isaiah (xxix. 1 f.) which most probably means "altar-hearth".

The Vestments of the Priests and High Priest (xxviii and xxxix). In strict accord with the detailed description of the tabernacle and its appointments is the elaborate description of the garments of the priests, especially of the high priest. That the function of the priest is that of a mediator is indicated clearly by the fact that the names of the tribes are to be engraved on the shoulder pieces of the ephod and on the stones of the breastplate of judgment. The high priest is to "bear the names of the children of Israel in the breastplate of judgment upon his heart, when he goeth into the holy place, for a memorial before the Lord continually" (xxviii. 29).

Apparently Aaron and his sons were chosen for this signal honour because Aaron was the brother of Moses (xxviii. 1) and because he had been Moses' spokesman (iv. 14–16), just as his great sin of apostasy was forgiven because of Moses' intercession (Deut. ix. 20). The setting apart of the Levites was on a quite different basis: it was the reward of loyalty (Exod. xxxii. 26 ff.; Deut. xxxiii. 8 f.). The Urim and Thummim are not described. Many suppose that they were sacred "lots". This is favoured by the fact that decision by lot is often referred to in the Bible (e.g. the land was divided by lot among the tribes).

The consecration of the priests is described in chapter xxix. It is to last for seven days (cf. Lev. viii–x). It is noteworthy that this account concludes with a brief description of the *continual* burnt offering (verses 38–46). The offering of *one* lamb morning and evening (cf. Num. xxviii. 1–10) for *all* Israel is very impressive. It indicates in a striking way that *quantitatively* the offerings required by God were negligible. He did not need them (Ps. l. 12; Acts xvii. 25). The words of Micah vi. 7 propose the *pagan* idea of sacrifice only to reject it utterly.

Reviewing these elaborate instructions for the construction of the tabernacle and its worship, we observe four noteworthy features: (i) *The Practical*. The tabernacle was to be a portable sanctuary, and it was made at Sinai. The materials used in its construction were such as the people had or could obtain (Exod. xxxv. 5–29). The gold, silver, and brass came from Egypt, as did also the fine linen and the dyes that were used. The goats' hair and rams' skins probably came from the flocks; the seal—or porpoise—skins, from the Red Sea; the shittim or acacia wood, from the peninsula of Sinai. Where gold was used, it was usually simply a gilding. Boards of solid gold would have been too heavy to move, even if the cost had not been prohibitive. Apart from the utensils used in the sanctuary, only the mercy-seat with its cherubim and the candlestick were of gold. The weight of the latter with its utensils was a talent. The silver of the half-shekel tax was the ordinary "money" of the people. Brass (bronze) was extensively used in the manufacture of vessels and utensils of every sort. (ii) *The Artistic*. This appears in the beautiful symmetry of design in the tabernacle and its appointments. The gold and silver and brass, the fine linen of the curtains, the elaborately embroidered hangings or veils, made this sanctuary a thing of "glory and of beauty". It was the worthy model for the glorious temple of Solomon. (iii) *The Symbolic*. It is obvious that there is a marked appropriateness in the various appointments of the tabernacle. But there has been much difference of opinion as to the extent to which symbolism is to be discovered in it. The holy of holies was a perfect cube (10 by 10 by 10). It is natural to see in this the type of the New Jerusalem, of which "the length and the breadth and the height of it are equal" (Rev. xxi. 16). Since gold was the most precious metal known to the ancients, it was highly proper that it should be used for nearly everything connected with the tabernacle itself; while brass, a much less valuable metal, was used for everything connected with the outer court and its furnishings. In this way a sharp and important distinction was made between the court of the people and the sanctuary of the Lord.

It was eminently appropriate that the mercy-seat should be of pure gold. But it would be a mistake to draw the inference that gold represents Deity in manifestation, and wood represents humanity. For the mercy-seat was pre-eminently *the* place of expiation (*kapporeth*). Consequently, such an interpretation of the symbolism would mean that it was only in His divine Nature that Jesus made atonement for sin. But such was not the case. The Deity and the humanity were joined (not merged) in the one divine Person. It was His Deity which gave infinite value to His sacrifice. But it was only in His human Nature that Jesus could suffer and die. The use of pure gold may show the special sacredness of the mercy-seat. But if we try to press the symbolism further, we may be involved in serious difficulties.

The use of silver is especially interesting. It represented, not a freewill offering, but a tax. This is probably the reason that it was silver, since silver was the "money" of the people, and we may assume that a half-shekel was within the means of all. The total was 100 talents and 1,775 shekels. The talents were used to make the sockets on which the golden boards and the pillars of the veil rested. We might call them the foundations of the tabernacle. The silver is called redemption money. We might be tempted to think of Ephesians ii. 20 and Revelation xxi. 14. Yet we must remember that it could not be said of Israel of old, any more than it can be said of us, that they were redeemed with "silver or gold". The entire generation which paid the half-shekel tax perished in the wilderness because of disbelief and disobedience. In this respect the silver levy was like circumcision. The paying of it was an act of obedience; but it did not (any more than did circumcision) secure of itself the salvation of the one who paid it.[1]

---

[1] We have already seen that this silver levy shows especially clearly that the figures for the census, as given elsewhere, are to be taken just as they stand. For the total of 100 talents at 3,000 shekels the talent gives 600,000 half-shekels, which with 1,775 shekels makes up the total of 603,550.

The same may be said regarding the colours used in the hangings and in the garments of the priests. Blue, purple, and scarlet are the three most often mentioned, and usually in combination. The one most often used alone is blue (violet). It is used for the robe of the high priest (Exod. xxviii. 31), and every Israelite is to have a thread or cord of blue in the fringe of his robe that he may "remember all the commandments of the Lord to do them" (Num. xv. 38). The fact that blue is the colour of the sky would make it suggest heavenly things. But when we turn to Numbers iv. 6–13 it is difficult or impossible to find any symbolism in the use of these colours. Purple is often called the royal colour. But the only place where it is mentioned alone (verse 13) does not suggest this. Nor does the use of scarlet (verse 8) suggest sacrifice. The study of symbolics is interesting and instructive. But it is full of difficulty; and it is easy to lose one's way in it.

(iv) *The Religious.* As we have seen, the whole pattern of the tabernacle is designed to emphasize the fact that God dwells *amid* but *apart from* His people. He is invisible, unapproachable in holiness: His people are sinful and may not enter His holy presence. His blessings must be mediated by a priesthood. Only the priests can offer sacrifice for sin on the great altar of sacrifice. Only they may enter the holy place and burn incense there. Only the high priest may enter the holy of holies. Thus the holiness of God, the sinfulness of man, the necessity of mediation by the priest and atonement by the blood of sacrifice are vividly presented to the mind of the worshipper.

A striking illustration of the way in which the religious and symbolic may enter into the minute details of the worship is to be found in the ritual of the sin offering as described in Leviticus. Ordinarily the blood of the sacrifices was sprinkled round about the altar of sacrifice (i. 5, 11, iii. 2, 8, 13) or poured out at the side of it (i. 15). But in the case of the sin offering the ritual was varied in a significant way. When presented by an individual (iv. 27–35) the priest was to put the blood with his finger upon the horns of the altar of sacrifice and pour out all the rest at the bottom (base) of this altar. The "common people" (laity) could not pass beyond the court. So the atoning blood did not pass beyond the court. The same applied even to a ruler. But if the high priest sinned, he was to bring the blood into the holy place, to sprinkle it seven times with his finger before the veil, put it on the horns of the altar of incense, and pour out the rest at the base of the altar of sacrifice in the court (iv. 6 f.). He ministered in the holy place. Consequently atonement must be made for him in the holy place lest he defile it. The same ritual was to be observed when the "whole congregation" sinned, apparently because the nation as a whole was a "kingdom of priests and a holy nation". A further distinction was that the bodies of the animals whose blood was presented in the holy place were to be burned, not on the altar of sacrifice but "without the camp" (iv. 12, 21, viii. 17, ix. 11, xvi. 27) in the place where the ashes from the altar were regularly placed (vi. 11). This was of course observed in the ritual of the Day of Atonement (Lev. xvi. 27); and Hebrews xiii. 11 points out that "Jesus, that He might sanctify the people with His own blood, suffered without the camp". In this the law of sacrifice, even in its most minute detail, is shown to have symbolic and typical significance. On the other hand the regulation that the sacrifice be slain on the "north side of the altar" (i. 11; cf. iv. 24, 33) may be devoid of any special symbolic or ritualistic significance. Only where such significance is stated in the Bible itself or is clearly implied or to be inferred from other passages, are we entitled to insist on a special meaning.

The observance of the sabbath is emphasized in connection with the commands for the making of the tabernacle (xxxi. 13–17, xxxv. 1–3). This is noteworthy. The construction of the tabernacle was not an ordinary task. It was a pious service, a religious duty. But this was not to mean that work on the sanctuary might lawfully be performed on God's holy day of rest. There were certain duties which were required on the sabbath (cf. Matt. xii. 5 with Num. xxviii. 9 f.). But these were definitely matters of worship. This suggests quite plainly that the secular business of the Church should not be transacted on the Lord's day.

Apostasy.

The Book of Exodus records an event which is significant for the whole future history of God's people, both Jewish and Christian, because it illustrates their proneness to apostasy. The murmurings at the Red Sea (xiv. 10 f.), at Marah (xv. 24),

in the wilderness of Sin (xvi. 2), at Rephidim (xvii. 2 f.), had
been occasioned by the trials through which they had passed,
and illustrated their human frailty. But at Sinai they had
entered into solemn covenant with Jehovah to be His peculiar
people, and had heard His voice declare the Ten Commandments. Apparently they had nothing to complain of but
Moses' prolonged absence. Yet in this relatively brief interval
they sinned grievously against the God they had promised to
obey, and broke the Law which He had given them.

"Up make us gods" (xxxii. 1). It is significant that while
there was only one calf, the word *Elohim* as applied to it is
construed as a plural (verses 4, 8, 23). This may be because the
bull was the symbol of more than one Egyptian deity. Consequently their sin is described as both idolatry and polytheism.
It was a flagrant breach of both the First and the Second
Commandment; also of the Third, since they were exhorted
to regard this calf as representing the gods who had brought
them out of Egypt, an act of sovereign power, performed by
Jehovah alone and represented as a judgment on these very
gods. Aaron's attempt to whitewash the whole abominable
transaction by proclaiming a "feast to Jehovah" was, even if
sincerely meant, an attempt at religious syncretism which
should be a warning to all students of Comparative Religion.

"They have turned aside quickly" (xxxii. 8). The deliverance
from Egypt, the awe-inspiring giving of the Law at Sinai, and
the solemn ratification of the Covenant were all quickly forgotten. The Israelites had been living for generations in a
polytheistic and idolatrous environment; and it was not easy
to throw off its spell and return to the pure monotheism of
Abraham. In Egypt, more than in Babylon, the distinction
between animals and men was largely broken down. The
Egyptians represented their gods as having the heads of
animals or as wholly animal; and they regarded living animals
as sacred to them. Hence the cult of the bull (*apis*), later
called Serapis.

"And Moses took the tabernacle" (xxxiii. 7-11). This passage
is clearly intended to state how the worship of God was conducted during the interval between the ratification of the
Covenant (xix. 1), or perhaps even from the time of the
Exodus, and the completion and dedication of the tabernacle
(xl. 1 f.). This interval was nine months or a year. The words

"and Moses took" (Authorized Version) suggest that Moses removed the tent from the camp because of the sin of the people in connection with the golden calf, as an evidence of God's displeasure with Israel. But the verbs in the Hebrew are frequentative (cf. Revised Version, "now Moses used to take") and imply that this was Moses' regular custom, the procedure which he regularly followed when he had communion with God. Since the tabernacle, which was to guard the sanctity of the God of Israel so carefully, was not yet constructed, Moses was wont to take the tent which he called the tent of meeting (tabernacle of the congregation) and pitch it outside the camp. Apparently this happened often; and the removal of the tent and the appearance of the pillar of cloud above it when it was pitched and the Lord spoke to Moses there, indicated to the people that God was with Israel, but also separated from them, and that Moses was His mediator. Priests and Levites had not yet been appointed. So Joshua, as Moses' servant, was placed in charge of the tent, where Moses apparently kept the Tables of the Law, when they were given to him. The critics who regard the entire description of the construction of the tabernacle, with which chapters xxv–xl are mainly concerned, as belonging to the priestly document P which they assign to the exilic or post-exilic period, hold that that elaborate tabernacle never existed and that the tent described in these verses is the only one which existed during the Sinaitic period; and they point out that it was so small that Moses (and Joshua) could carry it out of the camp. But there is no conflict when this narrative is understood as referring merely to the time before the tabernacle was constructed and erected by Moses. Regarding that tabernacle we are told again and again that it was constructed "as the Lord commanded Moses". Regarding this little tent we are told quite plainly that Moses used it before the tabernacle was constructed.

Exodus xxxiii. 25–9. The obedience of the Levites on this occasion was the reason for their setting apart to the service of God (Deut. xxxiii. 8–10).

Exodus xxxiv. 29. *Moses' face shone* (i.e. gave out rays or horns). The rendering of verse 33, "and *till* Moses had done speaking", should be "and when" (cf. Revised Version). Moses veiled his face, not because the people were afraid of him (they were afraid, but they returned to him, verses 31, 35), but that the people might not witness the gradual vanishing of the heavenly aura (2 Cor. iii. 13), which was the visible evidence that he had come forth from the presence of the Lord of glory (Exod. xxiv. 16–18).

We cannot read the history of Israel correctly unless we recognize and do full justice to the sinful tendency which is so emphasized in the Bible. This means that we cannot infer from the conduct of the people at any given time the nature and extent of the laws which had been given to Israel for their observance (John vii. 19). The fact that they were given the Law at Sinai was no guarantee that they would keep it. The fact that they broke or ignored its precepts is no proof that they did not have them. Moses warned them plainly what would happen (Deut. xxxi. 29, 30). Joshua did the same (Joshua xxiii. 15 f.). The "discovery" of the book of the law in the days of Josiah (2 Kings xxii. 8) is simply an example of revival after apostasy. Israel is stiff-necked and rebellious; and they are constantly rebuked for it by the prophets.

Our Lord (Matt xxiii), Stephen (Acts vii. 52), Paul (1 Cor. x) point this out most plainly. Their crowning sin was the rejecting and slaying of their Messiah. It is one of the most glaring errors of the higher criticism that its advocates assume that they can determine from the conduct and practices of Israel just how much or how little knowledge of God's will had been made known to them. Failure to keep the Law of Moses is no proof that the Law is not Mosaic. It is proof that the people failed to live up to the light that they had received through Moses. This was the great sin of Israel of old. It is the even greater sin of the Christian Church which has received also the grace and truth that came by Jesus Christ (John i. 14).

Finally, it is to be noted that tragic apostasy is made the occasion for the proclaiming of the Name of the Lord (xxxiv. 5–7). In the light of this wonderful revelation of the essential Nature of the God of Israel, the startling proposal made in xxxii. 7–14 will appear in its true perspective. God is both more righteous and more gracious than His servant Moses. Yet He tests Moses now, as He had tested him at the bush, by a proposal which was really a challenge to Moses' love of his people.

LEVITICUS[1]

THE THIRD book of the Law is called by the Jews *Wayyiqra'* ("And called", from the opening sentence: "And the Lord called unto Moses." This name is quite appropriate, because it serves to remind us of the fact that the book is largely made up of commandments and ordinances given to Moses for the people of Israel. "Called" is used only in i. 1. But about thirty times we read "and the Lord spake (said)". Seventeen chapters in the Authorized Version begin in this way.

Usually the one addressed is Moses. Three times Aaron is named with Moses (xi. 1, xiv. 33, xv. 1), and once Aaron alone is addressed (x. 8). While the book might be called a manual for the priests, who are mentioned nearly 200 times in it, it is noteworthy that about half of these disclosures of God's will are addressed to the people: "Speak unto the children of Israel", which makes it clear that all of these commandments are of vital concern to the people, despite the fact that in their observance and enforcement the priest plays an important and often an indispensable rôle. But the regulations for the day of atonement are intended especially for Aaron as high priest (xvi. 2). Chapter xvii is for both priests and people; chapters xxi and xxii are especially for the priests.

The only persons mentioned by name are Moses, Aaron, Aaron's four sons, and two near relatives (x. 4). The place is Mount Sinai. This is expressly stated four times (vii. 38, xxv. 1, xxvi. 46, xxvii. 34). The words "out of the tabernacle of the congregation" (i. 1) form a connecting link with the account of the erection of the tabernacle just concluded in Exodus xl.

The statement that these revelations were made at Sinai dates this legislation in a general way. The sojourn in Egypt

[1] The name "Leviticus" is taken from the Greek (LXX) Version. It is inaccurate and misleading, since the Levites, as distinguished from the priests, are only mentioned in one passage (xxv. 32–3) in the entire book.

95

and the deliverance from bondage there are mentioned repeatedly, which may suggest that it was quite recent (e.g.
xi. 45, xviii. 3, xix. 34, 36, etc.). The entrance into possession
of the land of Canaan is spoken of as future (xiv. 34, xviii. 3,
xix. 23, xx. 22, xxiii. 10, xxv. 2). As in the case of Deuteronomy,
the setting is definitely Mosaic. The first and the only precise
date is the mention of "the eighth day" (ix. 1), which followed
the "seven days" of consecration of the priests (viii. 33, 35; cf.
Exod. xxix. 35). These days are apparently to be counted
from the day of the setting up of the tabernacle (Exod. xl. 2),
which was the "first day of the first month" of the second
year, at which solemn function Moses officiated without the
help of Aaron (xl. 35). The consecration of the priests was
performed by Moses (Exod. xl. 12; Lev. viii. 6).

The consecration of the priests is described in detail in
chapter viii. In some respects it is a repetition of what has
been recorded in detail in Exodus xxviii–xxix, just as Exodus
xxxv–xl tells in detail of the execution of the commands given
in chapters xxv–xxx. In the case of the priests, as in the case
of the tabernacle, there was exact compliance with what was
commanded Moses (viii. 29, 36). So on the eighth day (ix)
Aaron and his sons enter upon their sacred duties. Aaron
offers sacrifices for himself and for the people (verses 7, 8; cf.
xvi and Heb. vii. 27). Then the Lord signifies His approval
by appearing in glory (verses 6, 23), probably in the pillar of
cloud and in the fire which consumed the offerings. This was
the holy fire (verse 24) which was to burn perpetually and
never to be allowed to go out (vi. 12 f.).

Then there follows, apparently at once, one of the most
singular events recorded in the Pentateuch, the sin of Nadab
and Abihu. As is often the case, the facts are allowed to
speak for themselves. Nadab and Abihu, the two of the four
sons of Aaron who had with the seventy participated in the
solemn rite described in Exodus xxiv. 1 f., offered their incense
with "strange fire", i.e. with fire not taken from the altar of
burnt sacrifices, which the Lord had kindled (cf. xvi. 12). Why
they did this we are not told. But punishment was swift and
summary: "they died before the Lord". It was a most solemn
warning, given at the very beginning, that the only form of
service acceptable to God is the one which He has Himself
appointed. Their intentions, like Uzzah's (2 Sam. vi. 6) may

have been good, but good intentions were not enough. So grievous was their sin that Aaron and his two surviving sons were forbidden to show any sign of mourning (verse 6), and were severely rebuked for their failure to carry out the ritual requirements with exactitude (verses 16–20), despite the terrible judgment that affected them so intimately.

We have here a striking proof that God's thoughts and ways are not like man's (Isa. lv. 8). The congregation of Israel was very large (more than 600,000 adult males). The services of the tabernacle was elaborate and exacting. The duties of the priests were onerous, or could be made so. There were but *five* priests, Aaron and his four sons. Yet at the very outset two of the four sons were cut off for disobedience (Num. iii. 3 f.). Numbers do not count with God as they do with men (Judges vii. 2, 4). God is able to use few as well as many, or even better (1 Sam. xiv. 6). It is to be remembered, of course, that Aaron, who was about eighty-four years old, may have had several other sons, and all of his sons may have had several sons of proper age for service at the altar. But if such was the case, no mention of it is made. Numbers iii. 1–4 seems to indicate quite definitely that the total number of priests was three.

In view of the fact that the higher critics, despite the clear indications of Mosaicity summarized above, have been insisting for many years that Leviticus forms part of the "priestly" legislation (P) which they assign to the exilic and post-exilic period, it is important to note that the situation described in Leviticus is so totally different from that of the late period to which the critics assign the book, that it is difficult if not impossible to believe that such a situation as is here described could have been *imagined* in later times. It bears clear indications of being a record of actual fact.

The Levites at the time of the Exodus numbered 22,000 (Num. iii. 39), of whom 8,580 were between thirty and fifty years of age. The priests, so far as the record states, were but *three*. On the other hand, according to 1 Chronicles xxiii. 3 the Levites of thirty years old and upward numbered 38,000 at the close of David's reign; and the priests were numerous enough to be divided into twenty-four courses (1 Chron. xxiv). The relative size of these courses is not stated. But they must have been rather large, since the average for the four courses which returned with Zerubbabel was more than 1,000 each, a

total of 4,289 (Ezra ii). Yet the total for the Levites who returned is only seventy-four (341 with singers and porters
added). When Ezra returned he took with him some priests,
but a special effort had to be made to secure thirty-eight
Levites (viii. 15, 18 f.).

The reasons for this disparity cannot be discussed here. The
noteworthy fact is that according to the Pentateuch, which
professes to describe conditions in the time of Moses, the
Levites were very numerous, while the priests were extremely
few; while according to Ezra and Nehemiah, which profess
to describe the conditions in the exilic and post-exilic period,
the reverse was the case—the priests were numerous, and the
Levites (at least, the available ones) were comparatively few.
Jews who were writing fictitious history would hardly have
imagined conditions so totally different from their own. Far
less would they have invented the story of Nadab and Abihu.
If their aim was to glorify Israel's past, and especially the
beginnings of the priesthood in Israel, they would never have
invented such a tragedy as befell the family of the first high
priest just as he was entering upon the holy duties assigned
to his office.

The only other historical event recorded in Leviticus is the
blasphemy uttered by a half-Israelite (xxiv. 10–16) and its
punishment. When it took place we are not told. Having now
considered the historical setting of the book and the events
which it records, let us pass on to consider the laws which
form the greater part of it, and which are to govern Israel's
life and conduct as the holy people of the holy God throughout their generations.

I. SACRIFICES (i–vii). It is significant that Leviticus, which
follows immediately the account of the erection of the tabernacle, with which Exodus concludes, should begin with a
detailed description of the sacrifices by means of which the
Israelite is to obtain forgiveness of sins, and acceptance with
God, and communion with Him. We might say that it represents the worshipper as having entered the court of the tabernacle, and standing before the great brazen altar of sacrifice.
Thus, at the very outset, even before the priests are consecrated, who are to be the ministers of the altar, the nature of
these sacrifices is described, and it is made clear to him that

without the shedding of blood there is no remission (xvii. 11; Heb. ix. 22).

The sacrifices were of two kinds: those which involved the shedding of blood, and those that did not.

(i) The *Animal Sacrifices*. These may be classified as (*a*) burnt, trespass, and sin offerings; (*b*) peace offerings. In all of these the shedding and the ceremonial manipulation of the blood indicated their expiatory character. But there was an important difference between them. The entire flesh of the burnt offering was consumed on the altar. It signified the complete dedication of the individual or of the nation to God. Hence it was also called the whole burnt offering (*kalil*), also the *continual* offering (*tamidh*), when speaking of the offering of one lamb (two on the sabbath) morning and evening for the sins of the entire people (Exod. xxix. 38 f.).

Of the sin or trespass offering the flesh, apart from the portions burnt on the altar (e.g. iv. 8–10), was in some cases eaten by the priests (e.g. vi. 26, x. 12–15); in others it was burnt without the camp (e.g. iv. 11, 12).

In the case of the peace offerings, which implied, as the name suggests, that the offerer was in a state of peace with God, reconciled by sacrifice and obedience to His law, the offerer and his family were permitted to feast on most of the flesh of the offering (iii. 1–17, vii. 11–36; cf. Deut. xii. 5–7, 11 f., 17–19, xvi. 10 f.). This was a eucharistic feast, a feast of communion. The poor were to take part in it.

In the case of the animal sacrifices, the principle of substitution is stressed by the command that the offerer "put his hand" on the head of the sacrifice (i. 4, iii. 2, 8, 13, etc.). The principle of representation also appears in the provision that if the "whole congregation" sin, the "elders" shall offer the sacrifice on their behalf (iv. 15). It is to be noted that the sacrifices set forth three important features of individual and national worship: expiation, dedication, communion.

(ii) *Other Offerings*. Other things which made up the daily food of the people were offered by them in worship to God. But the bloodless offerings, e.g. the meal offering ("meat" offering in the Authorized Version is confusing), of fine flour with oil and frankincense, and the drink offering of wine, ordinarily accompanied the animal sacrifices, and owed their efficacy to them. Salt was to be used with all the sacrifices (ii.

13); and nothing leavened was to be placed on the altar (ii. 11). The same applied to honey. But leavened cakes were to be offered under certain circumstances (vii. 13).

The mention of "leavened cakes" (vii. 13; cf. xxiii. 17) is noteworthy. It seems designed to remind us of an important fact which may easily be overlooked. *Leavened bread* was the usual and staple food of the Israelites from patriarchal to New Testament times. The leaven made it wholesome and palatable. Consequently it is a mistake to assert that leaven always represented an "evil principle". For this would imply that except during the feast of Unleavened Bread the people were free to contaminate themselves with what was evil in itself or represented and symbolized it. Cf. Exodus xii. 34 f., which states definitely the reason the Israelites ate unleavened bread at the time of their flight from Egypt. This was quite different from the sacramental requirement. The fermentation produced by the leaven made it unsuitable for use in sacrifices which were to be placed on the altar. Hence this definite restriction in its use.

It was not God's purpose to make this sacrificial system burdensome to the people. The animals used most frequently were the lamb or goat and the bullock. But the poor might offer a very inexpensive animal, a dove or pigeon, and in extreme cases a bloodless offering might even be accepted, being placed on the altar where the bloody sacrifices were regularly offered (ii. 2, 8, v. 11–13). It will be recalled that the Virgin Mary offered for her cleansing the offering of the poor (Luke ii. 24).

II. THE PRIESTS (viii–x). These chapters combine the historical account of the consecration of Aaron and his sons, the tragic side of which has already been pointed out, with the rules regarding the consecration and duties of priests and high priests, which were to be observed by Israel throughout their generations. The priests' duties were threefold: to make atonement for the sins of the people by sacrifice (i–vii), to bless the people in the name of the Lord (ix. 22; cf. Num. vi. 23–7), and to teach the people the will of God and enforce the laws which He had laid down for their observance as a holy people set apart to his service (x. 11; cf. Deut. xxxi. 9–13). Moses, as the direct representative of God, consecrated Aaron and his sons by means of an elaborate ritual. Cf. xxi. 1–xxii. 16 for the special application of the laws of purity to the priests.

III. Uncleannesses which Barred from the Sanctuary (xi–xv). The people of the holy God must be a holy people. This is repeatedly stated (e.g. xi. 44 f.; Deut. vii. 6, xiv. 2, 21). They must avoid all defilement:

(i) *Through Unclean Animals* (xi). The distinction between clean and unclean animals goes back to a very early time (Gen. vii. 2). We observe also that the animals mentioned in Genesis as used in sacrifice were clean animals (xv. 9). Here we have general principles stated, and also definite animals named as clean or unclean. Thus, the bullock, the lamb, and the goat, are domestic animals bred and tended by man. Wild animals and birds that are predatory are unclean. The carcases of these animals, whether clean or unclean, are unclean and defiling. In some of the laws the hygienic principle enters quite obviously, in others not. Thus the swine, being at times a flesh-eating animal, would be debarred on that ground. But it is also a filthy animal; and the claim is made that in tropical and semi-tropical countries it is unwholesome as an article of diet. Deuteronomy xiv permits the eating of certain herbivorous wild animals.

(ii) *Uncleannesses of Women* (xii). While the Mosaic law recognizes that marriage is lawful for all (even the high priest was expected to marry), it treats everything related to sex relations, generation, birth, etc., as defiling. This was because sin has corrupted, not the individual only, but the race. The child is begotten in sin, despite the fact that marriage is divinely ordained. Psalm li. 5 states this general truth, and is not intended as any reflection on David's mother, save as a member of a fallen race. Consequently, purification is necessary. Several other factors may enter in, such as the protection of the health of the mother and child, recognition of the sacredness of blood, and the necessity of excluding all sexual rites and abuses from the worship of the sanctuary. The last is especially important because of the prominence given to sexual rites in the religions of Israel's neighbours.

(iii) *Leprosy* (xiii–xiv). The exact nature of this disease is uncertain. Some regard it as a supernatural judgment upon sin, especially the sin of sacrilege. It is sometimes called the "stroke" of leprosy (compare the cases of Miriam, Gehazi, and Uzziah). By others, leprosy is regarded as a disease which they connect directly with what is now known as leprosy, or with some other similar disease. It is remarkable, in view of the detailed account given in these chapters, that we read so little in the Old Testament about leprosy. From the fact that the priest is to decide whether the disease is or is not leprosy but that nothing is said about any means of healing, it has been inferred by some that it was incurable. This inference seems doubtful in view of the elaborate ritual provided for the cleansing of the healed leper, unless we are to infer that healing was regarded as a special act of God. Leprosy, because of its loathsomeness and the elaborateness with which it is dealt with as a pollution which must be removed from a holy people, may properly be regarded as a type of sin. David's prayer, "Purge me with hyssop and I shall be clean" (Ps. li. 7) suggests that he has the ritual for the cleansing of the leper in mind (Lev. xiv. 4–6).

(iv) *Uncleannesses of Men and Women* (xv). Here both normal and abnormal conditions are dealt with; and the general principle, the necessity of purification, is stressed.

IV. THE DAY OF ATONEMENT (xvi). This was a special day of atonement for sin for all Israel. None was exempt, not even the high priest who performed the ceremonies required. It was on this day only that the high priest was permitted to enter the holy of holies, which made it peculiarly sacred. Cf. the words "within the vail" (verses 2, 12, 15) with Hebrews ix. 7. Aaron must then offer sacrifice for himself (verse 6), for the people (verse 15), for the tabernacle itself (verse 33), and even for the altar of incense (verses 17 f., cf. Exod. xxx. 10) in the holy place. The entire ritual should be carefully studied. The bullock is Aaron's offering for himself and his house; the two goats are the offering for the people; the rams are an offering for both priests and people.

The ritual of the two goats involves a distinction which is important. The one goat is offered as a sin offering for the people, the other is sent into the wilderness to (or for) azazel. The word "azazel" is probably to be derived from a root meaning "go" or "go away"; and so would mean "dismissal or removal" (verses 10, 21 f.). Hence the rendering "scape-

goat" in the Authorized Version. The thought of the complete removal of the sins which have been atoned for by sacrifice seems to be intended. The sins of the people are to be con-
fessed upon the head of this goat, and then it is to be utterly
removed, to pass into oblivion (Mic. vii. 19; Ps. ciii. 12). It
has been claimed that azazel is here a proper name, and
refers to a demon of the desert as representing Satan. But
there is no proof of this. It seems more probable that as the
one goat represents expiation, so the other represents complete removal. It is to be noted that the day of atonement
was the only one on which fasting was required; they were
to "afflict their souls" (verse 31).

"And he did as the Lord commanded Moses" (xvi. 34). These
words are to be carefully noted, since they tell us definitely
that the day of atonement was observed at the appointed
time. This must mean that the apostasy at Kadesh did not
take place until after the day of atonement, nearly five months
after Israel left Sinai. The sin of rebellion or presumption
("the high hand", Num. xv. 30, Revised Version) was punished
by "cutting off"; and the generation of wrath was condemned
to perish in the wilderness. A ritual of atonement for "all"
the sins of the people (verses 30, 34) could not apply to them.
We may infer, therefore, from xvi. 34, that the regular ritual
of the tabernacle was in force for several months before it
was suspended by the apostasy. In general, then, Darby calls
attention to an important fact when he says: "There is no
proof that one sacrifice was offered; possibly the fixed ones
were; but Amos, quoted by Stephen, would say the contrary.
Those born in the wilderness were not circumcised, and
could not rightly keep the passover" (Synopsis, i, 286). But
it is to be noted that Darby's first sentence can apply only
to the time after the apostasy took place. This law is connected with the sin of Nadab and Abihu (verse 1) apparently
because the death of two of Aaron's sons for disobedience
was intended to serve as a solemn warning to Aaron against
any laxity or disobedience in the performance of his duties
when, six months later, on the day of atonement, he was to
enter the holy of holies for the first time.

V.—MISCELLANEOUS LAWS (xvii–xxvii). These chapters contain
a great variety of laws which Israel is to observe as the holy

people of their holy God. They will repay careful study, though our space will not permit us to discuss them. They are the requirement of God Himself. The words, "I am the Lord (your, their God)," occur nearly fifty times in these chapters (beginning at xviii. 2). Israel is to be holy, because He is holy (xix. 2, xx. 26, xxi. 8). He is the One who sanctifies them (xx. 8, xxi. 8, 15, 23, xxii. 16), and holiness is to be the constant and pervasive feature of their daily life. It is to enter into, and regulate, the most intimate and personal relations of their family and social life, and into their worship, both individual and national.

Chapters xvii–xx concern the people as a whole: "all the children of Israel" (cf. xix. 2). First the slaying of animals for food is dealt with (xvii. 1–9). The three classes of animals used in sacrifice are to be treated as peace offerings and slain at the door of the tabernacle. It is quite obvious that this law applied primarily to the period of the journeyings and sojourn in the wilderness. It is definitely modified in Deuteronomy xii. 15–24 to adapt it to conditions "in the land", a clear indication that Deuteronomy follows Leviticus, despite the claims of the critics to the contrary. Verses 10–16: in view of the sacredness of the blood, its use in expiation for sin, eating with the blood is expressly forbidden (Gen. ix. 4; Heb. ix. 22). Chapter xviii deals with sex relations, prohibited degrees, and unnatural vices. Neither Egypt nor Canaan is to be the norm for Israel in these matters (verse 3). Some of the things forbidden show the carnality and corruption in Israel with which the grace of God had to contend. Chapter xix deals with a great variety of subjects. Especially noteworthy is the command, "Thou shalt love thy neighbour as thyself" (verse 18; cf. verse 34), which Jesus called the "Second" Commandment and which sums up the contents of the second table of the Decalogue. A practical example is given in verse 10. Strict honesty is required (verses 35 f.). Chapter xx prohibits some of the most abhorrent practices of the Canaanites and supplements the laws of chapter xviii by prescribing the penalty for the sins there described.

Chapters xxi–xxii are for the priests. As the representatives of the Lord, they are to be particularly careful to avoid what is sinful; and they are to be free from physical blemishes and defects. The same physical perfection is required in the case of animals which are brought to the priests for sacrifice (xxii. 17–33). Chapter xxiii is addressed to "the children of Israel". It describes the "feasts" which are to be "holy convocations": the sabbath, passover, feast of unleavened bread, first fruits, weeks (or the fiftieth day, pentecost), trumpets, day of atonement, tabernacles. Cf. Exodus xxiii. 10–17; Deuteronomy xvi. 1–17. Chapter xxiv.: commands of various kinds; oil for the lamps to be provided by the people; the shewbread; punishment of the blasphemer, other sins; principle of exact justice as opposed to revenge (verses 19–20). Chapter xxv: the sabbatic year and the year of jubile. The former is referred to in Nehemiah x. 31. Jeremiah represents the Babylonian captivity as a sabbath rest for the land. It required the cancelling of debts and the release of Hebrew slaves (Deut. xv. 1–15). The law of the jubile was intended to do for the land what the sabbatic year did for debt and bondage, restore the original ownership as established by inheritance. There is no clear reference to its enforcement in the Old Testament (cf. Isa. lxi. 1–3; Ezek. xlvi. 17; Neh. v. 1–13). That the Israelites failed to enforce this law is only what might have been expected. But that such a law was invented and promulgated as Mosaic centuries after the conquest and distribution of the land under Joshua, seems absurd.

Chapter xxvi describes the blessings which are to follow the keeping of the Law (verses 1–13) and the curses which will as surely follow disobedience (verses 14–39). The four scourges— famine, wild beasts, sword, pestilence—appear frequently in the course of the later history (cf. Ezek. xiv. 21). Jeremiah and Ezekiel refer frequently to the "sword" (esp. Ezek. xxi). Then the way of pardon and return is pointed out as resting on the Abrahamic covenant (verses 40–5). Verse 46 is a kind of certification or attestation which may be regarded as applying to all the preceding chapters. Chapter xxvii deals with vows, tithes, and dedicated things. In view of xxvi. 46 it also receives its own certification (verse 34).

That this is to be a moral and not merely a ceremonial holiness, an actual separation from moral evil, is made clear by the ethical quality of very many of the laws. Leviticus xix. 18 gives us the second of the two great commandments which summarize the Decalogue: "but thou shalt love thy neighbour as thyself", a command which is followed by the solemn words, "I am the Lord". And in verse 34 this command is extended to include "the stranger that dwelleth with you"; and the reason is stated, "for ye were strangers in the land of Egypt", and the same high sanction given, "I am the Lord your God".

On the other hand, many of the sins which are prohibited cast a dark shadow on the picture, and suggest the terrible depravity of the human heart in its alienation from God. Yet, lest we be tempted to take too low a view of Israel's culture and morality, we must remember that some of the vices which are here condemned were the sins not only of so-called backward and primitive peoples, but also of the cultured nations of antiquity, of Greece and Rome in their golden age. Culture and morality do not always go hand in hand. "The tender mercies of the wicked are cruel."

The great lesson of the Book of Leviticus is that the holy God must have a holy people, and that this holiness must embrace the whole of life. The New Testament statement of this principle may be found in the words: "Whether therefore ye eat or drink, or whatsoever ye do, do all to the glory of God."

In view of the elaborateness of the laws recorded in Leviticus, it is important to remember that these laws were intended to govern the lives of an obedient and God-fearing people. They were not merely external and ceremonial or ritual. They were moral and religious and were intended to govern the "thoughts and intents of the heart". Those who claim that the ethics of the Old Testament are so inferior to those of the New that they cannot both have God as author, should remember that the Old Testament code set such a high standard that the people as a whole and as a rule were quite unable to observe it; and the history of Israel as recorded in the Bible is one of constant and flagrant disobedience to the will of God. The critics claim that these laws could not have existed in the days of Moses because they were not observed. According to the Bible they were both known and disobeyed; and it makes it the great sin of Israel for which the people were punished again and again, that this law was given to them at Sinai and that they disobeyed it or forgot it.

NUMBERS

THE title "Numbers" is taken from the Greek Version. It is appropriate, because of the emphasis placed on the first census of Israel by making it the first topic discussed. The book begins with that phrase which occurs so frequently in Leviticus, "And the Lord spake unto Moses."[1] But apparently because "And spake" might easily be confused with "And called" (their name for Leviticus) the Jews in later times referred to it by the phrase "in the wilderness" (*bemidhbar*) which immediately follows.

The Book of Numbers has four major divisions: I. Israel still at Sinai (i. 1–x. 10); II. From Sinai to Kadesh Barnea—Apostasy and Rejection (x. 11–xiv. 45); III. The Years of Wandering (xv. 1–xix. 22); IV. Events of the Fortieth Year (xx. 1–xxxvi. 13).

I. ISRAEL AT SINAI (i. 1–x. 10). The Numbering of the Twelve Tribes and their Camp is dealt with in chapters i–ii. The date given, the first day of the second month (verse 1) indicates that the arrangement is not chronological (cf. vii. 1, and especially ix. 1 ff.). The census is placed first because of its importance. Israel is not an unorganized and heterogeneous "mob". They are a distinct people, whose names and ages and tribal relationships are definitely known. We have seen that the total amount of the half-shekel tax (Exod. xxxviii. 25 f.) is identical with the figure given here in Numbers; and we have inferred from this that both tax and census were taken as of the same day, probably the day of the setting up of the tabernacle (Exod. xl. 2). It is also to be noted that the figures given in Numbers i–ii are round numbers, i.e. they are in thousands and hundreds (i. 25 is the one exception), which might allow for minor variations which would take place in the course of a few weeks or months.

The figures are interesting. Judah is much the largest of the tribes, considerably larger than its nearest rivals (Dan and

[1] It is even more frequent in Numbers, occurring over forty times, and at the beginning of sixteen chapters in the Authorized Version.

Simeon) and more than twice the size of the smallest (Benjamin and Manasseh). The total for each tribe is given, and then the grand total for the twelve. Then it is pointed out that the Levites have special duties, and are not to be included in this census.

Chapter ii groups the twelve tribes in four "camps", and states the position of the camps with reference to the tabernacle, and the relative order of each camp on the march. Not only are the figures given in chapter i repeated, but a total for each camp is given in addition to the grand total. It is interesting to note that, while chapter i follows the grouping by camps of chapter ii, in the order of march the camp of Judah is given precedence over Reuben. This is the first intimation of the leadership promised to Judah (Gen. xlix. 8–10).

In chapters iii and iv the Priests and Levites are numbered and their duties are stated. The brief account of the family of Aaron (iii. 1–4), in view of its position in the census, seems to indicate quite clearly that the priests, after the disobedience of Nadab and Abihu had been punished by death, numbered three and only three. The Levites are numbered, and presented to Aaron and the priests to be their servants and assistants (iii. 6). They number 22,000 males of a month old and upward. They are taken in place of the first-born males (Exod. xiii. 2, 15) of all the twelve tribes, who number 22,273, the difference being made up by the payment of five shekels each for the extra 273. The fact that the number of first-born is so small as compared with the total of 603,550 may seem remarkable. We must remember that we do not know exactly what is meant by first-born. For example, Aaron was the first-born *son* of Amram; but he was not the first-born in the sense of Exodus xxxiv. 19. Miriam was that. Jacob had four wives. In the sense of Exodus xxxiv. 19, four of his sons were "first-born" sons. Yet strictly speaking his first-born was Reuben (Gen. xlix. 3). We must assume that these very precise figures correspond with the actual facts, even if we cannot fully explain them.

It is especially to be noted that the duties of the Levites as given in chapter iv are such as were applicable, in general, only to the time before the Conquest and permanent occupation of the land of Canaan. Their duties are carefully defined in connection with the taking down of the tabernacle and its transportation (iv), but very little is said about their general duties (iii. 6–9; cf. xviii). The former duties were, of course, of vital and pressing interest (iv. 18 f.) when Israel was about to set out for Canaan. But after the Conquest they became relatively of secondary importance; and after the erection of the temple they ceased to be of anything but antiquarian interest. Yet it is these duties which are stressed.

This shows how definitely this record, which the critics assign to the time of the exile or later, reflects the Mosaic age. The same applies to the rules laid down for the encamping of the tribes and the order of march. The whole setting is Mosaic.

As is so often the case, the rules given for the order of march in chapters ii–iv are supplemented elsewhere by the account of the putting of them into effect (x. 11–36) as governed by the Cloud which betokened the Presence of God (ix. 15–23). Some of the details are uncertain. Thus, it seems to be implied that the ark was carried in the midst of the host (ii. 17, iii. 31, iv. 15, x. 21). On the other hand, the words "went before them" (x. 33) seem to imply that the ark was carried ahead of the host (Joshua iii. 3 f.). It is to be kept constantly in mind that we are dealing with a host of several million persons, whose camp must have been a square mile at the least, or even several miles, and whose line of march, unless they advanced on a very wide front, might have extended for miles. This must have involved many practical problems which are not dealt with except in the most general way.

An interesting question is posed by the specifications in chapter iv regarding the covering of the ark and all the sacred vessels of the tabernacle, that they might be safely carried by the Levites. Does this mean that the ark was always to be covered, except when in the holy of holies? Or are we to assume that on such a momentous occasion as the crossing of the Jordan (Joshua iii. 3) the people were allowed to see the ark itself? The words "when ye see the ark" (verse 3) would seem to imply the latter, although we may be expected to construe them in the light of Numbers iv. This may also be implied in 1 Samuel vi. 19. It would seem to be proper to make a distinction between what we might call a "ceremonial passage" of the ark on a solemn occasion, and the rules governing its removal from place to place when Israel journeyed. But the evidence is not decisive either way.

The Cleansing of the Camp is the subject of chapter v. The camp of the Lord is to be kept from defilement. Those unclean because of leprosy or an issue are to be removed from the camp where God dwells (verse 3). Various trespasses are dealt with, especially the ordeal for the woman suspected of unfaithfulness by her husband. It is called the "law of jealousies" (verse 29) and is stated with unusual fullness. It is mentioned here as a trespass which defiled the camp. But its nature as involving jealousy on the part of a husband indicates how disastrous to the whole life of the community is even the suspicion of marital unfaithfulness.

The Nazarite (vi. 1–21) was one who *separated* himself by certain duties or abstinences which he performed as a vow to God. This separation might be for a given time, or for life. The only person called a Nazarite in the Old Testament is Samson (Judges xiii. 5, xvi. 17). But Samuel was apparently also one (1 Sam. i. 11, 28). And Amos ii. 11 f. and Lamentations iv. 7 indicate that the practice was not rare in Israel. The greatest of Nazarites was John the Baptist (Luke i. 15).

The Priestly Benediction (vi. 22–7). Nothing is said as to when this blessing was to be pronounced (cf. Lev. ix. 22), which would seem to indicate that it was the regular form. The blessing is markedly poetic in form. It is made up of three couplets or double verses, in each of which the Lord is invoked, and the climax is reached in the word "peace". To pronounce this blessing is to "put the name of the Lord" upon His people (cf. Exod. xxxiv. 5–8).

The Dedication of the Altar (vii. 1–88) involved the presenting of identical gifts by the princes of each of the tribes. Since this ceremony began immediately after the dedication of the tabernacle, and lasted for twelve days, it was not completed until after the seven days of the consecration of the priests were ended. It is to be noted that the six wagons with the twelve oxen (to draw them) were given to the sons of Gershon and Merari, whose duty it was to transport the tabernacle, its boards and curtains and pillars, a further indication of early date. The repetition serves to emphasize the fact that all of the tribes contributed equally to the service of the sanctuary, and so had an equal right to worship there. Cf. Joshua xxii.

Moses' Unique Position (vii. 89) is referred to, apparently primarily with reference to the dedication of the altar, which has just been described. But it is stated in such a way as to indicate that it was here, i.e. at the tabernacle (but in the holy place and before the altar of incense) that the Lord revealed His will to His servant Moses. It shows Moses' unique position (cf. xii. 6–8; Deut. xviii. 15–19, xxxiv. 10). The fact that the Voice came to Moses as from One sitting upon or above the ark, accounts for the rendering mercy-seat (Luther: *Gnaden-stuhl*) for *kapporeth* or propitiatory which defines the mercy-seat as pre-eminently the place of expiation.

The Lighting of the Lamps (viii. 1–4) apparently refers to the first lighting of the lamps of the golden candlestick by Aaron after his official consecration to office.

The Cleansing of the Levites (viii. 5–26) naturally follows the consecration of the priests. They are to be the servants of the priests. Their period of service is to begin at twenty-five, and end at fifty.

The Passover (ix. 1–14) is the first as an anniversary feast. For it is celebrated a year after the departure from Egypt when Israel first kept the passover, and it is now observed at Sinai just a fortnight after the erection of the tabernacle. It is to be noted that provision is made for a delayed passover to be held a month later, for the sake of those unavoidably prevented from observing it at the usual time. This exception is made to meet a definite situation (verse 6) which would arise again and again. It illustrates both the sanity and humanity of the Mosaic legislation.

Guidance for the Journey to Canaan (ix. 15–23). The fact that Israel was supernaturally guided by means of the pillar of cloud and of fire, is stressed by the heaping up of concrete instances which form the basis for the statement of verse 23.

The Silver Trumpets (x. 1–10). The Pentateuch mentions three kinds of trumpets, which were to be used by the priests to summon or to warn the people (to assemble, set forward, prepare for battle, etc.). It is to be noted that there is no mention of the use of musical instruments or of singing in connection with the service of the tabernacle as ordained through Moses. The great antiquity of music and musical instruments is attested by the Pentateuch itself, which refers it to the antediluvians (Gen. iv. 21) and incidental references appear in patriarchal times (Gen. xxxi. 27). Moses sang a song of triumph after Pharaoh's army was destroyed (Exod. xv; cf. Num. xxi. 17); and Miriam led the women in a choral response. Moses also taught the people a "song" (Deut. xxxi. 19) to be sung throughout their generations. Yet hymnody had apparently no part in the regular worship; and the words for "praise", "give thanks", etc., which occur so often in the Psalms, are scarcely found.

Why the service of song should have been introduced by David and not by Moses we do not know. But this fact is a remarkable proof of the early date of the Pentateuch. For if the Pentateuch were post-Davidic and the "Priest Code" (P) post-exilic as the critics claim, it is safe to say that its authors would have definitely referred to that service of song with which they had been familiar for centuries in the worship of the temple, and would have represented it as Mosaic. Otherwise they must treat "Davidic Psalmody"as quite as much an invention of later times as the "Mosaic Law". When the critics reject the Mosaic authorship of the Pentateuch, they involve themselves in all sorts of difficulties and contradictions.

II. FROM SINAI TO KADESH BARNEA (x. 11–xiv. 45). Israel sets forth from Sinai (x. 11–36). The tabernacle having been erected and its worship instituted, the passover having been celebrated and the census taken, after a sojourn of nearly a year at Sinai (Exod. xix. 1), Israel sets out for Canaan. First a summary statement is given (verses 11–13), then a detailed account of the procedure (verses 14–28), which has already been described in chapters ii–iv, is given, and the whole is followed by a concluding summary (verses 33–6). Moses, we are told, invoked the divine blessing at the beginning and ending of each stage of the journey. The invitation to Hobab[1] to accompany Israel on their journeys and the reason given, "thou mayest be to us instead of eyes", does not suggest any

[1] Hobab was apparently Jethro's son and Moses' brother-in-law (cf. Revised Version text and margin at Judges i. 16, iv. 11). He may have remained with Moses when Jethro departed (Exod. xviii. 27; cf. 2 Sam. xix. 33–8). "Raguel" is simply a different English spelling of Reuel which has come down through the Greek (LXX). The Hebrew has the same word here and in Exodus ii. 18.

lack of confidence in the divine guidance by the pillar of cloud and of fire. There were many ways in which an experienced desert sheik might be of service to Israel in journeying through the desert. The Bible constantly teaches us to make use of all the ordinary means which God has provided, while at the same time depending upon Him to supply whatever else may be needful.

The murmurings of the people are recounted in chapter xi. Their ingratitude and forgetfulness frequently drew down upon them the displeasure of God, and taxed to the utmost the patience of Moses. They were tired of the manna (cf. Exod. xvi. 14–36) and wanted flesh to eat. The passionate outburst of Moses (verses 11–15) shows how human he was, and how great a burden he had to bear. Cf. for similar examples Job x. 8–22; Jeremiah xx. 7–18; Jonah iv. 1–8. The summoning of the seventy elders and bestowal upon them of the spirit of prophecy shows how greatly Moses needed help for the performance of his arduous duties (cf. Acts vi. 1–7). The demand of the people for meat is granted, but they are punished for their greed. The words of verse 31, "as it were two cubits *high* upon the face of the earth", certainly do not mean that the quails were piled up all around the camp to a height of a yard in a circuit of five or ten miles. It probably means either that they flew so low that they could easily be caught or killed, or that in some places their bodies were piled up to that height as a maximum. But it is definitely stated that immense quantities were caught (verse 32); and the people were condemned to eat quail for a whole month (verses 19 f.) as a punishment for their lust (verse 33).

The Challenge to Moses' Authority (xii. 1–15). Moses also had difficulty with his immediate family. Being older than Moses (Exod. ii. 4, vii. 7), Miriam and Aaron resented Moses' pre-eminent position. The pretext was his marriage to the Cushite woman. Zipporah cannot be meant (cf. Exod. xviii. 1–6); and the event referred to was apparently quite recent. We know nothing of the circumstances; but the fact that Moses is not rebuked by God indicates that his act was lawful. Miriam seems to be mainly responsible, and is severely punished. The seriousness of the issue is shown also by the word "suddenly" (verse 4). Either Moses was too kind-hearted to deal severely with his next of kin (verse 3), or he was too "afflicted" (the Hebrew word may mean both "meek" and "afflicted") to stand up for himself as he should have done. So the Lord acted suddenly and vindicated Moses' authority by word and deed. Moses' unique position is made clear (verses 6–8; cf. vii. 89, also Exod. xxv. 22, xxxiv. 29; Deut. xxxiv. 10 f.). Moses was over the "whole" house of God (verse 7), but as a servant, not as the Son over His own house (Heb. iii. 1–6).

While Israel is still in the wilderness of Paran (xii. 16, xiii. 3, 26), the spies are sent out by Moses at the command of God (Num. xiii. 2), but also at the request of the people (Deut. i. 22 f.). They are sent out as a "fact-finding" body, it being assumed that their report cannot be other than favourable. An absence of forty days gives abundant time for the most thorough investigation. The report is favourable as to the land, but unfavourable as regards the possibility of conquering it. Caleb's answer to the latter is brushed aside.

Disobedience and Its Results (xiv). A night of weeping hardens them in the decision not to attempt to possess the land. Caleb and Joshua protest in vain, but despite all that Caleb and Joshua can say, the people refuse to advance, and even propose a return to Egypt. This sin of disobedience is like the apostasy of the golden calf. Again the Lord threatens to destroy the entire nation (Exod. xxxii. 7–10) and again Moses intercedes (verses 13–21). But while he is successful, the punishment visited on the people is very severe. Of all those who were recently numbered at Sinai only two, Caleb and Joshua, shall see the land of promise (verse 30). Since no representative of the Levites or of the priests was included among the spies, it seems proper to infer that they were not included in this grievous sentence. (Note that Aaron's son Eleazar enters the land, and he assists Joshua in allotting it, Joshua xiv. 1.) Forty years, a year for a day, Israel is to wait outside the land, until the generation of wrath has perished. The tardy repentance of the people (verse 40 f.) is of no avail. To insist on going up when commanded not to, is as sinful as to refuse to go up when commanded to do so. So they are allowed to suffer defeat at the hands of their worst enemies, the Amalekites (cf. Exod. xvii. 8–16). The day of opportunity was for them past for ever.

III. The Years of Wandering (xv–xix). An interval of about thirty-seven years is covered by these few chapters, yet only one important event is recorded, the sedition of Korah, Dathan, and Abiram (xvi). It is noteworthy that a group of laws which are to govern the conduct of Israel as the people of God should be introduced immediately after the verdict of exclusion from the land has been pronounced on the generation of wrath. The words, "Speak unto the children of Israel, and say unto them, When ye be come into the land of your habitations, which I give unto you" (xv. 2), are full of pathos and promise, when we remember that they are addressed to a generation that cannot enter because of unbelief, and can apply only to their children.

Additional Laws Regarding Sacrifice (xv). The words just quoted, "when ye be come into the land", seem to imply that the priestly ritual of the tabernacle was in abeyance during the wilderness period (cf. Amos v. 25 f.; Acts vii. 42 f.). The laws given here presuppose residence in the land. Note the reference to the sojourner (verses 15 f.). Sins of ignorance can be atoned for (verses 24–9); but sins of presumption (literally "of the high hand") cannot be atoned by sacrifice. They imply a wilful, defiant attitude which refuses to obey God. Such a sin was the "gathering sticks" on the sabbath (verses 30–6). The refusal to go up and possess the land was another example of this sin. On the other hand Israel went out of Egypt "with a high hand" (Exod. xiv. 8; Num. xxxiii. 3), as an act of high defiance of Pharaoh and all his hosts.

The Uprising of Korah, Dathan and Abiram (xvi) was very serious, since it involved a large number of influential men (verse 2). Korah and his followers, being Levites, resented the superior rights of the priests (verses 8–11). The Reubenites resented the failure of Moses to bring them to a land flowing with milk and honey (they had refused to go up and possess it!) and they accused him of making himself a "prince" (verses 12–14). The severity of the punishment (verses 15–35) led to a murmuring of the whole congregation which was punished by a plague. The seriousness of this rebellion is clearly the reason for the affirming of the special rights and duties of Aaron and his sons and of the Levites in chapters xvii–xviii.

With a view to confirming Aaron in his office and duties,

the sign of the budding rod is given (xvii). The priests and
Levites are confirmed in their duties (xviii). The priests are
to receive certain portions of the sacrifices for their own use.
The Levites are to receive a tithe of their increase from all
the tribes, and to give a tenth of it to the priests.

Purification from uncleanness by means of the ashes of the
heifer (xix) is a perpetual statute for Israel. The uncleanness
referred to here is especially that due to contact with a dead
body. Death, being the punishment of sin and the antithesis
of that life which is given by the living God, is defiling, and
purification is necessary.

It is significant that chapters xv–xix, except for the two
historical incidents referred to above, ignore the years of
waiting completely. There is no mention of dates or chronological sequence. They fill in the time of enforced waiting, as
it were, with laws and provisions for the government of the
people when the time comes for them to enter and possess
the land.

IV. THE FORTIETH YEAR (xx–xxxvi). The date given in Numbers xx. 1, "in the first month", is so indefinite that it is
important to observe that this is the beginning of the fortieth
year since Israel left Egypt, and consequently the last of the
years of exclusion from the land for unbelief. It is plainly
stated that this period was to be forty years (xiv. 33 f.); and
the preparations for the conquest of Canaan indicate clearly
that this event is imminent (verse 14). So apparently the writer
considered it unnecessary to name the year (cf. Joshua iv. 19).
That it is the fortieth year is shown also by the fact that
Aaron's death (verses 23–9) is stated in the itinerary of chapter
xxxiii to have occurred in that year (verse 38). It seems as if
the writer wished to pass over the long years of wandering as
quickly as possible.

We have seen that chapters xv–xix mention only two historical events—the sedition of Korah and his associates, and the
case of the man gathering sticks on the sabbath. Neither of
these events is dated. Apart from this, these chapters are, quite
significantly, devoted to the announcing of laws which are to
govern the people when they have taken possession of the
land. Disobedience had been followed by apostasy; and the
extent of the apostasy is indicated by the fact that the basic

law, the sign of the covenant, circumcision (cf. Gen. xvii; Exod. iv. 25, xii. 48; Lev. xii. 3), was not observed during this period (Joshua v. 5). This would indicate that the people neglected or were debarred from the worship which centred in the tabernacle. Amos, as we have seen, describes it as a time of apostasy (v. 25 f.; Acts. vii. 42 f.).

"And the people chode with Moses" (xx. 3). Since this is the beginning of the fortieth year, and preparations are about to be made for the conquest of the land promised to the fathers, it is tragically significant that the history of it begins with murmurings that suggest the old generation (Exod. xvi. 2 f.; Num. xi), and imply also that the new generation which is so soon to take up the task their fathers have forfeited through unbelief, differs very little from the old. The account of the smiting of the rock at Meribah ("strife") resembles in some ways the event which had taken place nearly forty years before (Exod. xvii. 5–7). But here Moses and Aaron are guilty of a sin of presumption or disobedience (verse 12) which has bitter results for both of them.

Edom's Refusal (verses 14–22). If Kadesh is correctly identified with *Ain Kudeis,* Edom must have claimed territory extending thirty or forty miles west of the Arabah ("the uttermost of thy border"). Moses makes his request as modest and courteous as possible. He asks simply for permission to pass through Edom by the regular highway or caravan route (the king's way). They will not even ask for water. In case they should drink of the water of the wells, they will pay for it. What could be more reasonable than this!

Refusal was due partly to fear (cf. xxii. 3–6), but more perhaps to hatred and hostility. Note Moses' words, "thy brother Israel", and the definite pledge of friendly intentions. This refusal is the beginning of a bitter hostility between the two nations which is to continue for centuries. David's conquest of Edom was ruthless (1 Kings xi. 14 f.); and the burden of prophecy concerning Edom is almost wholly denunciatory (cf. Ezek., Jer., Amos, Obad.). It is the New Testament which opens the door of hope wide to Edom (cf. Acts xv. 17 with Amos ix. 12).

The Death of Aaron (verses 23–9) apparently followed quite soon upon the announcement of punishment. This was not Aaron's first act of disobedience (cf. Exod. xxxii). That act of gross apostasy was forgiven because of the prayer of Moses (Deut. ix. 20). But for this act Moses is to suffer the same punishment as his brother.

Battle with the Canaanites (xxi. 1–3). If Mount Hor is *Jebel Madara*, which is about fifteen miles north-east of Kadesh, the phrase "way of the spies" suggests that Israel was still in the vicinity of Kadesh and that Arad the Canaanite expected Israel to attack from the south (cf. Num. xiv. 45). At the time of their first sojourn at Kadesh "Hormah" (destruction) had spelled disaster for Israel. Now it means disaster for the Canaanites.

The conquest of the East Jordan region (xxi. 14–35), a very important campaign, is described quite briefly, but it was an undertaking of great magnitude. It involved the skirting of Edom and Moab (cf. Num. xxxiii. 37–48); and the destruction of the kingdoms of the Amorite rulers, Sihon and Og. Moab and Ammon were not to be attacked since they were the children of Lot (Deut. ii. 9, 19).

The Brazen Serpent (verses 5–9). The people again murmur, and are punished by the plague of "burning" (from the same root as "seraph", Isa. vi. 2) serpents. The serpent of brass acquires special significance because of its typical character (John iii. 14 f.). Since the serpent here, as usually in the Bible, represents that which is evil and deadly, it cannot be that the serpent of brass represented a living serpent, such as those whose bite was bringing death to the people. Such a symbol could not inspire faith and bring healing. Rather must we think of the serpent as dead and the words "set on a pole" as meaning that it was to be represented as *impaled,* the usual meaning of "hang on a tree" in the Old Testament. Consequently it was to be by faith in One who could destroy him who had the power of death (the fiery serpent as representing that old serpent the Devil) that the believing Israelites were healed. To find serpent worship or sympathetic magic here is utterly to misinterpret the passage. 2 Kings xviii. 4 tells us that the brazen serpent was preserved for centuries in Israel as a sacred relic. But because it fostered idolatry Hezekiah had it destroyed.

"On the other side of Arnon" (verse 13). "Other side" is more frequently rendered "beyond" in the Authorized Version. It is an ambiguous expression, and its meaning varies according to the viewpoint of the writer. Here it apparently means the near or south side of the Arnon (cf. xxii. 1). It is pointed out quite definitely that while Moses was forbidden to attack the Moabites, he did not understand this to mean that he was to regard the territory which Sihon had taken from them, the land east of the Jordan between Arnon and Jabbock, as still Moabite territory, despite the fact that he so describes it in verse 20. Consequently, before crossing the Arnon, he sends messengers to Sihon; and only when Sihon refuses permission for Israel to pass through in order to enter the land of Canaan does Moses proceed to take possession of his land east of the Jordan and of the territory of Og to the north. This also indicates quite clearly that Moses did not regard these lands east of the Jordan as included in the territory Israel was entitled to by virtue of the promise to the fathers. It was Sihon's refusal of passage into Canaan which led to the conquest of all of this territory, and to the request of the two and a half tribes that it be assigned to them.

The student should turn to a "relief" map and study carefully, if he is not already familiar with it, the remarkable configuration of this entire region. The tableland, as we may call it, east of the Jordan averages more than 2,000 feet above sea level. The hill country of Galilee, Ephraim, and Judaea is also quite mountainous. In between is the great "fault", the Jordan valley. At the waters of Merom, the Jordan is only a few feet above sea level. At the Sea of Galilee it is nearly 700 feet below sea level, at the Dead Sea nearly 1,300 feet below. Consequently the Arnon, the Jabbok, and other lesser streams both east and west of the Jordan cut deep fissures in the mountainous plateau. To "go up" to Jerusalem from Jericho is a climb of more than 3,000 feet! An ordinary map fails to give the reader any idea of these interesting and important matters.

Balak and Balaam (xxii–xxiv). "In the plains of Moab on this side Jordan by Jericho" (verse 1). This tells us that Israel is now at the very gates of the land of promise. *Moab* is to be taken in the sense indicated above. This was Moabite territory taken from Sihon. "On this side" is almost exactly the expression rendered by "on the other side" in xxi. 13.

Israel has refrained from attacking Moab and Ammon, has conquered Sihon and Og, and is now ready to cross the Jordan.

But Balak is perhaps ignorant of the reason (Deut. ii. 9) and, being appalled by the fate of the Amorites, feels convinced that he will be the next victim (Deut. ii. 25). Being in despair because of the size of the hosts of Israel (xxii. 5, 11, xxiii. 10, 13), he seeks supernatural assistance. Taking counsel with "the elders of Midian" (xxii. 4, 7) he sends for Balaam to Pethor (probably Pitru on the Euphrates, some 300 miles away). What the connection between Moab and Midian was at this time we do not know. Who Balaam was, we cannot say. He must have been a famous diviner or seer, since Balak sent twice, and to such a distance, to enlist his services (verse 6). Whether Balak knew that Balaam claimed to be a worshipper of the Lord (xxii. 18), we are not told. But in his first refusal Balaam says expressly: "the Lord refuseth to give me leave to go with you" (verse 13). How then can Balak expect Balaam to prevail on the God of Israel to curse His own people? Balaam has foreseen the difficulty and consulted the Lord; and the Lord has definitely refused to curse Israel. Yet Balak, now certainly aware that Balaam professes to be a servant of Jehovah, refuses to take No for an answer; and Balaam, although assured that Jehovah will not curse His own people, shows an obstinate and hypocritical determination to go.

Balak's conduct is perhaps due to desperation. He knows his own god, Chemosh, cannot help him; so he turns to the far more powerful God of the people of whom he stands in terror. Truly the wisdom of the wicked is but folly.[1] Balaam clearly is influenced by cupidity and greed, though he professes the contrary (verse 18). Having shown his eagerness to go, despite the warning that the whole object of such a journey is utterly vain (verse 12), the Lord sends him (verse 20), even compels him to go (verse 35), but always with the

---

[1] It may be that Balak hoped that Jehovah was still angry with Israel. He knew, perhaps, that their forty years' sojourn in the wilderness was a punishment for disobedience. So he may have hoped that Jehovah was not yet appeased and would not favour the attempt of His "nomad" people to seek to conquer territory to which, in his opinion, they had no right. According to the Moabite Stone, Mesha explained the fact that Omri of Israel "afflicted Moab many days" as due to Chemosh's being "angry with his land"; and in Judges we read frequently that Jehovah "sold" his people into the hands of their enemies to punish them for disobedience and apostasy.

warning that he will not be allowed to do what Balak has
sent for him to do. It is an amazing story of perversity,
stupidity, and obstinacy.

"And the Lord opened the mouth of the ass" (verse 28). The
speaking of the ass and the appearance of the angel are
represented as actual happenings. 2 Peter ii. 16 supports the
literal interpretation of this amazing event. We are told that
the ass "saw" the angel each time that he barred the way and
that Balaam did not see him. We are also told that the ass spoke
because the Lord opened her mouth and that Balaam finally
saw the angel because the Lord opened his eyes. The encounter is a definitely supernatural encounter and "the dumb ass
speaking with man's voice" is an important feature of it. These
are represented as actual happenings and we should not try
to explain them away. We may note, however, a close resem-
blance to Paul's vision on the Damascus road. It was a real
vision. Paul actually saw and spoke with the risen Christ.
But it was a vision which meant nothing to his companions
(Acts ix. 7, xxii. 9).

The Four Prophecies (xxiii–xxiv) all serve to illustrate in a
striking way the fact that true prophecy, even when uttered
by an unwilling and a wicked man, is a "word of God", a
revelation of the will of God. God's conditions and His purpose, "Thou shalt not curse the people: for they are blessed"
(xxii. 12), and "only the word that I shall speak unto thee,
that thou shalt speak" (verse 35), both define and limit the
words uttered by Balaam.[1]

The first of the prophecies (xxiii. 7–10) starts out with the
basic proposition, stated as a rhetorical question, that the seer
cannot curse where God has not cursed, and, affirming the
favourable status of Israel, closes with the wish to share it.
Balak sees in it just the opposite of what he was hoping for.

The precautions taken by Balak to prevent the second prediction from being favourable to Israel, show both the folly
and absurdity of heathen superstition. Balak believes Balaam
must at least see the people he is to curse. But to see too much

[1] The seven altars, bullocks, and rams may indicate the survival in
Moab of some elements of the faith of Abraham (Gen. xxi. 28 f.). But
the sacredness of the number seven was rather extensively recognized in
ancient times. It figured, for example, in Assyrio-Babylonian magic and
religion.

of them may terrify him and prevent him from cursing them. A mere glimpse may be sufficient. But this clever device has no effect.

In the second utterance (verses 18–24) Balaam makes it plain that the purpose of God to bless Israel is unchangeable, because of the very nature of God Himself. It is also unalterable because God "hath not beheld iniquity in Jacob" (verse 21). These words, which may account for Balak's hope that the Lord might be prevailed on to curse Israel, are of course to be taken in a relative and not in an absolute sense. God *has* found iniquity in Jacob. The generation of wrath that has perished for disobedience is sufficient proof of this. What is meant is that, *so far as Moab is concerned*, Israel is innocent of all wrongdoing. Israel has not invaded Moab's land; and Moab has no occasion to seek the punishment of Israel. Balak's fear and his hate are alike unwarranted.

The following rendering of verse 23 is probably to be preferred to that given in the Authorized Version: "Surely there is no enchantment in Jacob, neither is there any divination in Israel." Heathen rites (cf. Deut. xviii. 9–14) have no place in nor power against God's people. "At the time (or, from time to time) it shall be said to Jacob and Israel what God is going to do (or, will do)." Prophecy will be a distinct and distinctive feature of the religion of Israel.

So the prophecy closes with a more glowing picture of the future prosperity of Israel.

In the third prophecy (xxiv. 3–9) Balaam predicts the establishment of a kingship in Israel, and he concludes with words which suggest the covenant promise to Abram (Gen. xii. 3), a reference to which may actually be intended in view of the conditions laid down for Balaam before he starts on his ill-fated journey (xxii. 20); and when Balak's wrath bursts forth and he upbraids Balaam for failing him so utterly, Balaam reminds him of this all-important condition (xxiv. 13). It is terrible to think that a man who could utter such words as these and seemingly with such sincerity and earnestness, could fall as Balaam fell (xxxi. 16).

The last prophecy (verses 15–24) which Balaam utters, as it were on his own initiative, though of course under divine constraint, is far more definite than the others. It is definitely Messianic, and expands the allusion to the king and kingdom in the third prediction. The star and sceptre may refer primarily to David of the line of Judah (Gen. xlix. 10); but the prediction has its complete fulfilment only in great David's greater Son (Matt. ii. 2). The ships from Chittim point forward to the Roman conquest of Bible lands. In fact, there is a close connection between this prophecy and some of the prophecies of Daniel (cf. Dan. xi. 30). Both came out of a heathen environment. Yet the difference between this venial and vicious seer and the man "greatly beloved" is so great that we might marvel that there should be any connection between them. The connection is that both Balaam and Daniel uttered the words which *God gave them to speak*. So, having uttered great words of promise concerning Israel, cast off and spurned by Balak, empty-handed, Balaam "returned to his place". But we are still to hear from Balaam.

The Sin of Baal-peor (xxv). It is hard for those who live in Christian lands, where the Bible determines to some extent at least the norm of ethical conduct, to realize the terrible plight of those in heathen lands who can easily be *better* than their religion, whose religion drags them down instead of lifting them up. This chapter is an appalling example of this terrible state of the heathen world. Having failed to destroy Israel by Balaam's curse, their enemies seek to corrupt them by means of the licentious worship of Baal-peor, obviously in the hope that Jehovah's curse will follow such immorality and apostasy as they seek to bring about. Again Moab and Midian are mentioned together (verses 1, 6, 17). Yet the sin seems to be treated as especially Midian's (xxxi). Comparing xxv. 1 f. with xxxi. 15 f., we can hardly avoid the inference that Moab and Midian are almost synonymous terms. Joshua xiii. 21 suggests that the term "Midian" may have been used of the inhabitants of the lands between Arnon and Jabbok, whose mixed population recognized the overlordship of Sihon.

"And Israel joined himself unto Baal-peor" (verse 3). It might seem as if all the lessons of the years of wandering had been forgotten. A plague is sent which devours 24,000. Aaron's grandson Phinehas "turned away" the wrath of the Lord. The Bible constantly tells us of what single individuals did in times of general decline and apostasy. Hosea (ix. 10) points to Baal-peor as a conspicuous example of Israel's proneness to apostasy.

The Second Census (xxvi) is a census of the new generation (verses 64 f.). That is the reason it is taken. It differs from the census of Numbers i–ii in several respects. Thus, it deals largely with tribal families, which are entirely ignored in the first census. While the grand total differs only very little (a fraction of one per cent), the figures for the tribes vary considerably. Most significant is the loss of Simeon (59,300 reduced to 22,200). Does this mean that Simeon was the one most deeply involved in the sin of Baal-peor (cf. xxv. 14)?

In view of the amazing increase of Israel during the sojourn in Egypt, it is significant that during the forty years there was a slight decrease in the total for all the tribes. Seven increased in number, five decreased. The greatest gain was made by Manasseh, the greatest loss by Simeon. As at the first census the Levites were numbered separately. They increased slightly in numbers.

It is emphatically stated that none of those who were included in the first census were numbered in the second, except Caleb and Joshua (verses 63–5). Whether this statement applied also to the Levites is not made perfectly clear. The words of xiv. 29 taken in connection with xxvi. 2 seem to indicate that it referred only to the twelve tribes, since they were numbered at the age of twenty or older, while the rule for the Levites was one month or older. The fact already mentioned that Levi had no representative among the spies also favours this conclusion as does the fact that Eleazar, the son of Aaron, took his father's place and assisted Moses in making the census. Eleazar was at least thirty years old when he was consecrated a priest shortly after the erection of the tabernacle (Num. iv. 3; cf. Lev. viii–x).

The Daughters of Zelophehad (xxvii. 1–11). The question of inheritance has been touched upon in connection with the census, and the fact mentioned that Zelophehad had five daughers but no sons (xxvi. 33). Since the land is to pass by inheritance, this raises an important problem which is further dealt with in chapter xxxvi and in Joshua xvii. Note how Naboth speaks of "the inheritance of my fathers" (1 Kings xxi. 3).

Moses is to die and Joshua is to succeed him (verses 12–23). Moses, like Aaron, must die outside of the land. But Moses is permitted to bring the people as far as Jordan, and to see the land which he may not enter. Here the account is quite impersonal, but elsewhere (Deut. i. 37, iii. 23–6) Moses gives expression to his poignant regret, and reminds the people that they were to blame. Moses is to place "(some) of the honour" which has belonged to his unique office upon Joshua. But the fact that Joshua must inquire the Lord's will through Eleazar the priest shows the vast difference between him and Moses.

The elaborate account which is given in xxviii–xxix of the offerings for the feast days acquires special significance, if, as we have reason to believe, the observance of all these stated offerings and ceremonies was suspended during the years of wandering. Some of it is a repetition of what has already been given (Exod. xxix. 38 f.; Lev. xxiii). The offerings for the seven days of the feast of tabernacles are given only here.

Chapter xxx supplements Leviticus xxvii, since it deals with the vows taken by women. These vows may be annulled by one who has authority to do so. Otherwise they are as binding as a man's.

Vengeance on the Midianites (xxxi). This chapter records the carrying out of the command, "Vex the Midianites, and smite them" (xxv. 17). It is to be the last act of Moses (verse 2), which indicates that it is not an act of revenge, but a solemn judgment of God on flagrant moral evil. After performing it, the warriors were commanded to purify themselves. It may be noted that in the division of the spoil the priests received one-tenth of the portion of the Levites. It was an immense booty. The army of Israel numbered only 12,000 and not a man lost his life, despite the fact that the Midianites must have outnumbered them many times over (the booty included 32,000 virgins). This must mean that the Lord fought for Israel in a very special and wonderful way. The extreme severity in dealing with the captives must be regarded as primarily punitive, vengeance for the awful sin of Baal-peor. It was in accord with the command to exterminate the Canaanites (Deut. xx. 16–18) and its object was to safeguard Israel from the abominations of these nations (cf. Gen. xv. 16).

The Fate of Balaam (xxxi. 8). They slew the five kings of Midian; "upon their slain" is the literal rendering; and

"Balaam the son of Beor they slew with the sword". They slew him because he was the instigator of the sin of Baal-peor (verse 16). Did Balaam really believe that he could bring about the destruction of Israel by corrupting them with evil which their God hated and would surely punish? Did he think he could do this and himself escape the swift and righteous vengeance of the God whose words of blessing had fallen so recently from his own unwilling lips? Or had Balaam's hypocritical and half-hearted devotion to Jehovah simply turned to blind and devilish hatred which sought revenge at any cost? We cannot fathom the depths of the human heart. The Bible is the greatest of all manuals of psychology. The psychiatrist has invented the word "schizophrenic" to describe certain abnormal mental states. The word figures in criminal medicine to-day. The Bible has a quite simple word to describe this morbid condition. It is "double-minded"; and it tells us that the double-minded man is "unstable" in all his ways. Balaam is a tragic example of such a man; and his terrible fate, like that of Ananias and Sapphira in the New Testament, is a solemn warning to all who are tempted to sin against God and resist His Holy Spirit.

Reuben, Gad, and Half-Manasseh (xxxii). How Reuben and Gad came to be the possessors of so much cattle we are not told. Israel had flocks and herds when they left Egypt (Exod. xii. 38); and they had recently acquired vast herds from the Midianites. But why the reason given by Reuben and Gad applied to them more than to the other tribes we cannot say, unless it be that they had given themselves especially to the breeding of cattle during the long years of wandering. Their request, with which half-Manasseh associates itself, is granted, on condition that they take their full part in the conquest of the land beyond Jordan. This they agree to do; and they carry out their promise.[1] But their settlements east of the Jordan gradually led to estrangement between them and the other tribes (cf. Joshua xxii); and the fact that these tribes were willing to remain outside the land, shows how little the Abrahamic covenant meant to many of the seed of Abraham.

[1] According to Joshua iv. 12 f. they sent 40,000 men across the Jordan, which was somewhat more than one-third of their total strength as given in Numbers xxvi. 7, 18, 34. This must have been regarded as fulfilling the condition imposed by Moses.

The Itinerary of Israel (xxxiii). As an historical document this chapter is of very great importance. It is especially to be noted that Moses is declared to have *written* it, a fact which has definite bearing on the Mosaic authorship of the Pentateuch. The journeys total forty-two. They may be grouped as: Egypt to Sinai (verses 3–15), Sinai to Kadesh, including the years of wandering (verses 16–36), Kadesh to Shittim (verses 37–49). The Israelites were at Kadesh at least twice: when the spies made their report (xiii. 26) and at the beginning of the fortieth year (xx. 1). Most of the stations mentioned in verses 16–36 are not given elsewhere, since chapters xv–xix give no itinerary of the wanderings.

The Land to be Thoroughly Conquered (xxxiii. 51–6). The "driving out" of the inhabitants of the land is necessitated by the sinful idolatries of the people, their "abominations"; and every evidence of their debasing religion is to be destroyed. It is necessary for the moral welfare of Israel. If Israel fails to do this, "I shall do unto you, as I thought to do unto them" (verse 56), a solemn warning which Israel failed to heed.

The Allotment of the Land (xxxiv). This makes no mention of *tribal* allotments, which are made by Joshua after the conquest of the land (Joshua xiii–xxi). "Mount Hor" (verse 7) may seem confusing, since it suggests the mountain where Aaron died (xx. 23). But it is clearly in the north. The word "Hor" is from the same root as "mountain" (*har*); and it may have been used of several conspicuous hills or mountains (cf. Num. xxxiii. 32). Joshua and Eleazar are to allot the land, with the aid of ten of the princes. Caleb, the faithful spy, represents the tribe of Judah.

The number and location of the Cities of the Levites and Cities of Refuge (xxxv) is given only in general. It is noteworthy that not a single city is mentioned by name. This indicates that the conquest is still future.

The right of women to inherit in the absence of a male heir comes up again for settlement (xxxvi). The general provision of chapter xxvii is safeguarded by the qualification that such women (again it is the daughters of Zelophehad) must marry within their own tribe. An inheritance shall not pass out of the tribe. The reason so much importance attaches to the daughters of Zelophehad is, as pointed out above, simply that their case involved principles of basic importance for an econ-

omy in which property rights were determined by inheritance.
The application of general rules and principles to specific and
exceptional cases may be at times both difficult and compli-
cated.[1] It is with such a problem that the Book of Numbers
concludes.

[1] It would be a mistake to attach special importance to this law on
the ground that it enabled Jesus to claim the throne of David through
His mother. The genealogy of Matthew i is declared to be that of
"Jesus Christ, the son of David, the son of Abraham", and it is traced
through Joseph who is expressly called "son of David" (verse 20; Luke
ii. 4). This must mean that Jesus was son of David as the legal son
and heir of Joseph (by adoption). Whether the genealogy in Luke is
also a genealogy of Joseph or gives the ancestry of Mary is not entirely
clear. It may be that Mary was also descended from David (cf. Rom.
i. 3; 2 Tim. ii. 8 and Acts ii. 30). But if it was through Mary that
Jesus' descent was determined, it would be strange that there is no such
statement in Matthew or Luke (that she was descended from David) as
is made in both Gospels regarding Joseph.

DEUTERONOMY

THE GENERAL character of Deuteronomy[1] is indicated by the opening words, "These are the words which Moses spake unto all Israel on this side Jordan". The book is largely composed of addresses made by Moses. In them Moses speaks in the first person; and his name appears only in the narrative portions (e.g. iv. 41, 44 f.). They were delivered to "all Israel", while Israel was "on this side Jordan". That is, they are Moses' farewell to Israel, uttered just before his death and in anticipation of the conquest of the land then to be undertaken by Joshua. Consequently, they have both the backward and the forward look. They are full of reminiscence and anticipation, of warning and exhortation. They are at times intensely personal, and reveal Moses' great love for Israel and his deep concern for their future welfare.

The "all Israel" to whom they are addressed is the generation that has grown to manhood and full responsibility during the nearly forty years that have elapsed since their fathers made the great refusal and were condemned to perish in the wilderness for unbelief and disobedience (i. 32, ii. 14, v. 3, xi. 7, xxix. 1–5). No man ever addressed an audience under more impressive circumstances than did Moses; and no audience ever had greater reason to give heed to the words of wisdom spoken in their hearing. Again and again we feel in them that passionate yearning and intense earnestness which are so fully in keeping with the circumstances in which they were uttered.

[1] The name "Deuteronomy" comes from the Greek Version. It occurs in xvii. 18 where the Authorized Version correctly renders by "copy". Deuteronomy is a "second law" only in the sense that these discourses were delivered in Moab at the end of the forty years and that in some respects they modify and adapt the laws given at Sinai to meet the new situation when Israel is in the land. In all essentials the Sinai laws and the Moab laws are the same. The Jews call this book "Words" (*debharim*) or "These are the words" (*elle debharim*) with which it commences.

No book of the Pentateuch—we might perhaps say, no book of the Bible—gives clearer indication of authorship and occasion than does Deuteronomy. Its situation and occasion are anticipatory of Moses' death and of the conquest which is to follow. Its speeches are definitely attributed to Moses. It is important to note this carefully. For this is the book of which the traditional (which is simply the Biblical) estimate has been most confidently and positively rejected by the critics. For more than a century, one of the foundations of the "critical" view of the Pentateuch and of the entire reconstruction of the Old Testament resulting from it, has been that Deuteronomy, at least in its present form, is not Mosaic, but dates from centuries after Moses' time, that it was composed more or less definitely with a view to bringing about the reform of Josiah in which the finding of the "book of the law" played so important a part (2 Kings xxii. 8, xxiii. 25). Those who hold this view do not hesitate, when they speak candidly and frankly, to call the Book of Deuteronomy a *fraud*, but they insist that it was "a *pious* fraud". By this they mean that it was written with the best of intentions, and that its authors are not to be judged by modern standards of literary honesty. But, just the same, it is to them *pseudo*-history, written with a laudable purpose. The reader should bear this in mind as he studies the book.

The analysis of the book is comparatively simple. It may be summarized as follows:

Introductory (i. 1–4).
Moses' First Discourse (i. 5–iv. 40).
Assigning Cities of Refuge (iv. 41–9).
Moses' Second Discourse (v. 1–xxvi. 19).
Blessings and Curses (xxvii. 1–xxviii. 68).
Sinaitic Covenant Reaffirmed (xxix. 1–xxx. 20).
Instructions for Priests, Levites, Joshua (xxxi. 1–29).
Moses' Song (xxxi. 30–xxxii. 52).
Moses' Blessing (xxxiii. 1–29).
Moses' Death (xxxiv. 1–12).

Deuteronomy emphasizes the Past and the Future. In studying this book, these two features should receive careful attention.

The Past. In Deuteronomy we have history "written with a purpose". Moses' appeals to the past are all for the purpose of counsel and warning. Because this past is so full of the most valuable lessons, Moses refers to it again and again. Consequently, just as Chronicles supplements Samuel–Kings, so we have in Deuteronomy an important supplement to the history given in Exodus–Numbers. So is it instructive to compare these accounts and see how they supplement and explain one another. A few examples will illustrate this. (i) According to Numbers xiii. 2, 16 f., 27, Moses sent out the spies at the command of God. According to Deuteronomy i. 22 f., this was done at the suggestion of the people, in which Moses heartily concurred: "and the saying pleased me well". These statements are not contradictory; they are mutually supplementary. (ii) ix. 20 explains why Aaron's life was spared after the sin of the golden calf; cf. Exodus xxxii. 15–35. (iii) Failure to mention Korah along with Dathan and Abiram (xi. 6) may be because of Numbers xxvi. 11. Since the sons of Korah were spared, the sin of their father, which is already a matter of record, is not alluded to again (cf. Ps. cvi. 17). Later they distinguished themselves as singers. Eleven psalms are attributed to them by the headings. The principle involved is stated in Deuteronomy xxiv. 16 (cf. Ezek. xviii for fuller treatment of the subject). (iv) The example of Edom in refusing to permit Israel to pass peaceably through her territory (Num. xx. 14–22) was apparently followed by both Moab and Ammon (cf. Judges xi. 17 f. with Deut. xxiii. 3, 4). Consequently, it would appear that it was not this sin, grievous as it was, but rather the hiring of Balaam to curse Israel, which was responsible for the different attitude toward Edom (xxiii. 7 f.). (v) The information which Moses gives regarding the past history of this region, both that which Israel is to possess and not to possess (ii. 4–24), is very timely for the situation in which Israel was placed; and it supplements the meagre information given elsewhere (e.g. Gen. xv. 19–21). It is of great interest also to the modern archaeologist.

The Future. Having definite reference to the situation and conditions which will follow the conquest, Deuteronomy naturally changes some of the legislation already given to make it applicable to the new situation. (i) The future reference of Deuteronomy is especially plain in connection with "the place which the Lord shall choose" to set His Name there (xii. 5, etc.). Thus the law with regard to the eating of flesh (Lev. xvii.

3 f.), which seems to imply that the slaughtering of domestic animals for food must take place at the tabernacle, is modified to permit the slaying of animals anywhere, provided the law regarding the blood is properly observed (Deut. xii. 15 f.). (ii) Such passages as xii. 12, 18 f. (cf. xiv. 27–9, xvi. 11, 14) indicate clearly that the importance of the Levites will diminish greatly after the settlement in the land. They are to be distributed in forty-eight cities (Num. xxxv. 6), and are to have no tribal inheritance. Hence, they will gradually be reduced to a dependent position comparable to that of the widow, orphan and stranger, since they will be largely dependent on the tithes which the people will pay only when they are living in accordance with that Law which Israel was so prone to forget and forsake. (iii) In representing the prophet (xviii. 20–2) as the proper substitute for those means which the heathen employed to discover the future, Moses suggests that in the future the prophet rather than the priest (Num. xxvii. 21) will be the principal channel of revelation, and that prophecy will gradually replace "inquiry" by Urim and Thummim (Ezra ii. 63; Neh. vii. 65). (iv) The kingship is definitely provided for (xvii. 14–20), but as belonging to the future. Israel had no king for centuries after Moses died. (v) The law of the "landmark" (xix. 14) was not required until the division of the land was to become a practical reality. It is merely, of course, an application of the Tenth Commandment, but a very necessary one (xxvii. 17).

THE INTRODUCTION (i. 1–4). The rather precise account of the circumstances under which Moses delivered the discourses which follow has occasioned much difficulty to Bible students. The words "after he had slain Sihon" and "on this side Jordan" indicate clearly that the forty years are ended (Num. xxxiii. 48 f.). On the other hand, some of the places mentioned in verse 1, and the explanation as to the length of the journey from Horeb to Kadesh-Barnea (verse 2), suggest that the occasion was the first arrival at Kadesh, when the conquest of the land seemed so very near at hand. Consequently, it has been suggested that the addresses which follow were delivered twice: first, before the great refusal, and then, with such changes as were advisable or necessary, at the end of the forty years, and in anticipation of the actual conquest.

ıt must be admitted that, but for the allusions to subsequent events (e.g. viii. 2, 4, 15 f.; xi. 6 f., etc.), the main addresses would have been quite as suitable for the one occasion as the other. But whether the statements in verses 1, 2 require or justify such an interpretation is not entirely clear.

THE FIRST DISCOURSE (i. 5–iv. 40) begins with the departure from Horeb. It mentions first the appointment of judges (verses 9–18), perhaps as a reminder of the fulfilment of the promise of the vast increase of the seed of Abraham which is to possess the land. Then it passes at once to the great refusal of the fathers (verses 20–46), and pointedly reminds them of its disastrous consequences (verses 35 ff.). This refusal is especially sinful, because this is the land which "the Lord sware unto your fathers, Abraham, Isaac, and Jacob, to give unto them and to their seed after them" (verse 8). This covenant (iv. 31, viii. 18) is referred to nearly thirty times in this solemn way, as *sworn* by the Lord. It is His oath (vii. 8), which He sware to the *fathers,* who are usually mentioned in connection with it. So the promise of possession was secured by the immutable oath of the immutable Jehovah. But it was also, for every generation of Abraham's descendants, conditioned on obedience. Dispossession or failure to possess was as certain to follow disobedience (ii. 14; cf. Num. xiv. 28–35) as possession was to follow obedience (iv. 37–40). Compare Genesis xviii. 14 with Jeremiah xxxii. 17, 27 for a striking illustration of this principle.

"Ye have compassed this mountain long enough" (ii. 3) refers to Mount Seir, and in general terms to the period of the wandering. It is to be carefully distinguished from the similar expression in i. 6, which refers to Horeb. Chapters ii–iii describe the conquest of the land east of the Jordan and the allotting of this land to the two and a half tribes (cf. Num. xxxii). The stipulation that they must aid in the conquest of the land leads naturally to Moses' first reference in Deuteronomy to the Lord's refusal to permit him to enter the land. Does it suggest a rebuke of their willingness to settle permanently outside the land?

In the impressive appeal with which Moses concludes this first discourse (iv. 1–40), he presses home to the people in the most solemn way that they are the unique people of the only true God, and that at Sinai He revealed Himself to them in a unique way: they saw no likeness, but they heard the voice of the living God declaring unto them His Law. Life and well-being are promised to them if they keep His commandments (iv. 1). They are neither to add to them nor diminish from them (verse 2). The possession of this Law is their greatest distinction (verses 8–14), and they are to guard themselves especially against idolatry (verses 15–30). They are to remember that their experience has been unique and unprecedented (verses 32–6), and that all this is because, and only because, the Lord "loved thy fathers, therefore He chose their seed after them" (verse 37). So it is their highest duty and privilege to obey this wonderful God, who has dealt so graciously with them.

It is to be noted that here, as frequently elsewhere, Moses, in addressing the people, often changes from the plural (e.g. iv. 1–8, 10–18, 20–3) to the singular (verses 9 f., 19, 24 f.) and vice versa, from "you" to "thou", and from "thou" to "you". The natural explanation is that he has both the nation and the individual constantly in mind, and addresses his words first to the one and then to the other. It may be, however, that he sometimes uses the singular pronoun collectively. We note also that he sometimes uses "we" (e.g. ii. 8), thus including himself with the people.

This wonderful address should serve as a much-needed tonic to all who are tempted, in these days of emphasis on "comparative religion" and "ecumenics", to forget that God "hath not dealt so with any nation" (Ps. cxlvii. 20) as He has dealt with "the Israel of God" (Gal. vi. 16) under the Old Covenant and under the New. The religion of the Bible, Old Testament and New Testament alike, is not just one of many religions, all of which answer more or less adequately to the needs of mankind. It is the only true religion for all mankind!

CITIES OF REFUGE (iv. 41–9). As if to relieve the tension of feeling which the solemn words of this discourse were calculated to produce, and also to prepare for the second, an historical and administrative matter of importance is introduced at this point. It is significant that only the names of the three cities east of the Jordan are given. This is indicative of early date.

Moses' Second Discourse (v–xxvi). There is no definite break in this lengthy discourse. But we may regard the first seven chapters (v–xi) as forming a major portion of it. Its great theme is the Decalogue and its significance for Israel.

"And Moses called all Israel" (v. 1; cf. i. 1). "The Lord our God made a covenant with us in Horeb" (verse 2). We are to remember that a considerable portion of the people who heard Moses speak had been present at Sinai at the first giving of the Law. Consequently, they are represented as the ones with whom the Lord really made the covenant, their fathers having forfeited their claim to it through disobedience. Their fathers had so completely repudiated it that it could properly be said not to have been made with them at all. "If ye will obey My voice indeed" (Exod. xix. 5) expressed the basic condition. They had pledged their obedience: "All that the Lord hath spoken we will do." But they had not kept the pledge (e.g. Num. xiv. 22). So they perished, while their "little ones", "their children" (verses 31, 33) are "alive this day" (Deut. v. 3); and it is to them that Moses speaks.

"The Lord talked to you face to face . . . saying" (verses 4, 5). This refers to their hearing the voice of God, since they saw no likeness or appearance (iv. 15–19). Then Moses repeats the Decalogue which the voice of God had proclaimed in thunder tones at Sinai. He begins with the "preface", as it has been called: "I am the Lord thy God, which brought thee out of the land of Egypt, from the house of bondage." Israel is never to forget the mighty acts by which God delivered them from bondage and claimed them as his peculiar people. They are doubly His: the seed of Abraham, delivered from bondage.

It is noteworthy that the only important difference between the form of the Decalogue as given here and that given in Exodus xx consists in the change in the "reason annexed" to the Fourth Commandment. Instead of the reference to Creation, we find the Bondage in Egypt referred to. Nothing could indicate more clearly the importance attached to this great deliverance, the great Old Testament type of redemption from sin, than this substitution which Moses makes in repeating the Ten Commandments, as the text of the "sermon", as we may call it, which immediately follows. It is clearly not a question of any change in the Decalogue itself. This funda-

mental law of Israel was already recorded on tables of stone
by "the finger of God"; and these tables as the "testimony"
of God were then in the ark. But Moses, for the purpose of
applying them pointedly to Israel's conduct in the coming
days, makes this change; he also makes several other minor
changes, perhaps to indicate that he is not quoting word for
word. After repeating the Decalogue, Moses again stresses the
awful grandeur and the uniqueness of that wonderful event
(v. 22–33).

"The living God" (v. 26) is not a frequent title. But it is a
significant one and its use is noteworthy (e.g. Joshua iii. 10;
1 Sam. xvii. 26, 36; 2 Kings xix. 4, 16; Jer. x. 10). Note also
the form of the oath, "as the Lord liveth" (e.g. Judges viii. 19),
and "as I live" (Num. xiv. 21, 28). This Living God differs
utterly from the idols of the heathen (e.g. Ps. cxv, cxxxv).
Because He is the living God, those who claim Him as their
God shall live also (Matt. xxii. 31 f.).

"Now these are the commandments, the statutes, and the
judgments, which the Lord . . . commanded to teach you"
(vi. 1; cf. v. 31). This piling up of synonyms or similar terms
is partly for rhetorical emphasis, and is characteristic of
Deuteronomy.

The First and Great Commandment: "Hear, O Israel, the
Lord our God is one Lord" (vi. 4). This is the great Old Testament affirmation of monotheism; and it is followed at once
by the exhortation, "and thou shalt love the Lord thy God
with all thine heart, and with all thy soul, and with all thy
might" (cf. xi. 1). This is the summary of the first table of
the Decalogue, and as such it is the "first and great commandment" (Matt. xxii. 38). The Jews call it the *Shema* ("Hear")
from the Hebrew word which introduces it. It is because
Jehovah is the one and only true God that He is a "jealous
God" (verse 15), and has a right to demand the exclusive
worship and obedience of His people.

"Love" expresses this demand in comprehensive terms; and
love is the only proper response to God's love to Israel. All of
God's gracious dealings with His people are the expression of
His love to their fathers (iv. 37) and to them (vii. 8). Joshua
makes the same appeal (Joshua xxii. 5, xxiii. 11; cf. Judges v.
31). It is sometimes claimed that in early times the religion
of Israel was national, ceremonial, external, that it was not

until centuries after Moses' time that religion became a personal matter to the Israelites. Deuteronomy flatly contradicts this claim. The relation between the God of Israel and His people, both the nation and the individual, is one of *mutual love.*

"With all thine heart, and with all thy soul, and with all thy might"—again we note the grouping together of words of related meaning for the sake of rhetorical emphasis. Cf. the repetitions in xiii. 4, and the seven "by"s of iv. 34. "Commandments which I command thee this day" is a phrase which occurs frequently and stresses the solemnity of the occasion (e.g. iv. 2, 40). "This day" occurs about seventy times in Deuteronomy.

"Shall be in thine heart: and thou shalt teach them diligently unto thy children" (vi. 6 f.). It was Israel's failure to obey this command which led to apostasy after apostasy. It is the failure of Christian parents to-day to study the Bible for themselves, and teach it to their children, which is responsible, directly or indirectly, for the ills from which Christendom is suffering to-day. Let a single generation grow up in ignorance, and all the precious heritage which the fathers have received will be lost to their sons. The Bible is the best practical handbook of psychology and pedagogy in the world!

"And thou shalt bind them" (verse 8). The Jews in later times took these words and those which follow with entire literalness; and they are rebuked in the New Testament for the extremes to which they carried this (cf. Matt. xxiii. 5). The context here in Deuteronomy and the use of these expressions in Exodus xiii. 9, 16 indicate that the language is figurative. But in this instance, as in many others, the figurative or spiritual meaning is far more important than the literal. This is a point which is often overlooked by those who insist that the literal meaning is to be adopted "wherever possible".

"For thou art an holy people" (vii. 6, xiv. 2, 21, xxiii. 14, xxvi. 19, xxviii. 9), a "special people" (verse 6), a "peculiar people" (xiv. 2, xxvi. 18; cf. Exod. xix. 5). The right of Israel to possess the land of Canaan is because of the Lord's choice of their fathers and His promise to them. It is not because they are or were "many" (they were very few, verse 7), or because they are "righteous" (ix. 5–29). It is because God is "faithful" (verse 9) to His promises. If they obey Him, conquest of the land and prosperity in it are assured. But if they turn aside after the abominations of the heathen, it will be done to them as they are about to do to these nations: they will be driven out of the land (iv. 25–8; cf. Gen. xv. 13–16). "The hornet" (vii. 20) may be meant literally; but it may also be a figurative reference to the king of Egypt, who wore the hornet as a symbol in his crown. If so, it implies that the Lord will use their recent oppressors to clear the land of its inhabitants (cf. Isa. vii. 18). Every evidence of idolatry is to be destroyed (verses 5, 25).

Chapters viii–xi contain exhortations and warnings, in which all of Israel's hopes and prospects are set in the light of the history of Israel's past. Israel is warned against cowardice, against self-righteousness and self-sufficiency, of the danger of apostasy through compromise with evil; and all of these lessons are enforced and illustrated by the record of God's dealings with them in the past; and the cogency of this appeal to that record lies in the fact that there are many present before him of whom it can truly be said: "Your eyes have seen all the great acts of the Lord which He did" (xi. 7). So Moses reminds them of their murmurings and apostasies at Sinai and elsewhere (ix. 8–x. 5); and declares: "Ye have been rebellious against the Lord from the day I knew you" (ix. 24). This charge is made again and again by the prophets (e.g. Isa. i; Jer. iv. 17; Ezek. ii; Lam. i. 18; Dan. ix. 5 f.; Hos. iv. 1). The fact that Moses interceded for Israel "forty days and forty nights" is especially stressed (ix. 18, 25).

He follows this exhortation with what we may call an appeal to their common sense. "And now, Israel, what doth the Lord require of thee, but . . ." (x. 12). The word rendered by "require" is usually rendered simply by "ask". It suggests the reasonableness of the terms upon the basis of which God deals with Israel. This is only too clear when we read them: "to fear the Lord thy God, to walk in all His ways, and to love Him, and to serve the Lord thy God with all thy heart and with all thy soul, to keep the commandments of the Lord and His statutes, which I command thee this day." And why? "For thy good." We may call it an appeal to enlightened self-interest. But it should have been a most powerful appeal. Israel had had so many proofs of the tragic folly of forsaking and disobeying their glorious covenant God. These words of

Moses find their echo in Micah vi. 6–8. We note also the significant coupling of the words "fear . . . love . . . serve". The holy law and inflexible justice of God inspire with fear; His mercy and grace call forth love; love finds expression in service! Sinai and Calvary! Many Christians do not realize the meaning of the Cross because they have never really faced the Law and its demands!

Moses concludes this portion of his address by referring to the very solemn ratification of the covenant which is to take place at Mount Gerizim and Mount Ebal and is fully described in chapter xxvii.

"The Place which the Lord your God shall choose" (xii. 5). For nearly forty years the tabernacle has been the centre of Israel's organization and worship. It is the place where the God of Israel dwells, even when His people have forsaken Him. Consequently, the conquest and permanent possession of the land of Canaan, which is constantly presented to the people as an immediate goal, raises a vitally important question. Will the tabernacle be located permanently in one place? Or, will it move about among the tribes?

The answer is twofold: all of the heathen shrines in the land of Canaan are to be utterly destroyed, and the people are to worship at one place, which will be, of course, where the tabernacle or its successor is located. This "place" is to be the one chosen "out of all your tribes" (verse 5). Its location is left undetermined, and is not to be determined until "the Lord your God giveth you rest from all your enemies round about, so that ye dwell in safety" (verse 10). Apparently these conditions were not met until the time of David (2 Sam. vii. 1). "Shall choose" is used nineteen times in Deuteronomy in speaking of this place. The fullest form is "the place which the Lord your God shall choose to place His name there". God will choose it, not the Israelites themselves.

It is perhaps significant in this connection that the words "tent" and "tabernacle", as applied to the sanctuary of the Lord, hardly ever occur in Deuteronomy. This suggests that Moses foresaw that under the changed conditions the tabernacle would give place to a more permanent structure, the temple. So he refers only to the "place". Such indefiniteness is quite appropriate on the lips of Moses. For Moses was a prophet, and true prophecy is marked by its silences and reserves quite as much as by its disclosures of the divine will. But would men writing in the time of Josiah, more than 300 years after Solomon's temple had been erected at Jerusalem, have confined themselves to such indefinite statements?

We have already noted that this intensely Mosaic book is the one which was the first to be denied to Moses by the critics. Their chief argument for this revolutionary claim is that centralization of worship at Jerusalem did not take place until the time of Josiah, not until after the fall of the Northern Kingdom and shortly before the fall of the Southern. This claim is largely based upon refusal to do justice to all the available evidence. The evidence shows two things very plainly: (i) that the establishment of the central sanctuary was not late but early in Israel's history; and (ii) that violations of this law were at times both numerous and flagrant. It is by ignoring the one and insisting on the other of these two facts that the critics arrive at their radical conclusions.

We observe the following points. (i) The idea of a central place of worship was established at Sinai in the tabernacle. (ii) The temple which Solomon erected was clearly intended (read Solomon's prayer in 1 Kings viii) to be the place of worship for all Israel. (iii) The account given of Hezekiah's reform in 2 Kings xviii which took place about a century before Josiah's, makes it clear that the removal of the high places and the command to worship at Jerusalem was based on the "commandments which the Lord commanded Moses" (verse 6). How drastic was the reform, and how serious was the situation which made it necessary is made clear by the words of the Rab-shakeh (verse 22). Here we have the two sides of the picture. We are told of the conditions which made the reform necessary, what the reform was, and that it was carried out according to the Law of Moses. The critics accept the account of the conditions as correct. They deny that they were a violation of the Law of Moses. That is, they accept the part of the evidence which agrees with their theory and reject the rest.

Other examples might be given to prove that the most serious error of the critics consists in their refusal to recognize what the whole course of Israel's history as recorded in the Bible makes so plain: that Israel's record was one of constant turnings aside from the Law of God which was given to them at Sinai. This led to abnormal conditions, which in some cases were condoned, "winked at" to use Paul's expression (Acts xvii. 30), as in the case of Hezekiah's failure to enforce all the requirements regarding the celebration of the passover which he made the climax of his reform (2 Chron. xxx. 15–22), or the use of altars by the faithful of the Northern Kingdom after the apostasy of Jeroboam (1 Kings xviii. 30 f., xix. 14).

How serious was this dislocation, as we may call it, is indicated by the fact that toward the end of the reign of David there were three places of sacrifice, each of which was more or less clearly sanctioned. (i) The ark was brought up to Jerusalem (2 Sam. vi. 12) and placed in a tent which David had pitched for it (verse 17). (ii) The tabernacle and the brazen altar were still at Gibeon (1 Kings iii. 4; 2 Chron. i. 3–6). (iii) David built an altar on Ornan's threshing floor (2 Sam. xxiv. 25). Apparently the ark never was in the tabernacle from the time it was carried out from Shiloh to battle by Hophni and Phineas (1 Sam. iv. 3, 4) until, more than a century later, it and the tabernacle were brought up and placed by Solomon in the temple (1 Kings viii. 4). When we think of the very explicit rules given in Exodus–Numbers for the tabernacle worship, and of the important place of the ark in that worship, we realize something of the disorder which entered into the worship of the Lord even in the days of David. This is not easy to understand. But it is far better to accept the explanation which the Bible gives of these abnormal conditions, than to take refuge in the radical theory which the critics propose, and which can only be established by rejecting express statements of Scripture regarding these matters.

"And there shall ye eat before the Lord" (xii. 5–7). These verses indicate clearly that this "place", after it has been chosen by the Lord is to be the centre of worship for Israel in the land, just as the tabernacle has been. The exceptions in verses 15–27 are intended to modify and adapt the law of Leviticus xvii to the changed conditions. They indicate very clearly that the law of Deuteronomy follows that of Leviticus; and not *vice versa* as the critics insist.

The importance of the law regarding the central sanctuary is again indicated in Deuteronomy xii. 29–31. Israel is to enter a land which will have heathen shrines everywhere (verses 2 f.).

The temptation to introduce Jehovah-worship at these pagan *sites*, even if the pagan *shrines* are destroyed, will be very great. But the law of the one altar established at Sinai and embodied in the tabernacle worship is not to be replaced by worship and sacrifice at many altars.

The Test of the True Prophet (xiii. 1–5). Prophecy goes back to the beginnings of Israel's history. Abraham is called a "prophet" (Gen. xx. 7); and the spirit of prophecy was manifested occasionally later (Gen. xlix; Num. xi. 25). But broadly speaking, prophecy belongs to the post-Mosaic period, especially to the time of the kingship. The phrase "The law and the prophets" (Matt. vii. 12) gives the historical sequence. Samuel, the "king maker", may be regarded as the founder of this distinctive movement; and the schools of the "sons of the prophets" probably originated largely with him. The sure test of true prophecy is to be its agreement with the basic law of Israel as set forth in the Decalogue. Even should the fulfilment of a dream or the performing of a sign or wonder seem to evidence its divine origin and authority, it is to be disregarded if it violates the Law. The Lord expects his people to "try the spirits, whether they be of God" (1 John iv. 1).

The Punishment of Apostasy (xiii. 6–18). The warrant and necessity for such severity as is commanded here is shown by the whole course of Israel's history. The nation must keep itself from all the abominations of the heathen, or it will suffer the same penalty as they for practising them. Only in utter separation from evil is there safety for Israel. Such severity as is here enjoined is both natural and appropriate in dealing in advance with the situation which will follow the conquest. But it is utterly unsuited to the time of Josiah, and sounds like a pious platitude or counsel of perfection, when we think how frightfully idolatry had prevailed in the days of Manasseh only a short time before Josiah's reform. Such a law, if rigidly enforced then, would have caused rivers of blood to flow. Yet, as far as we know, Josiah's reform, while drastic, was bloodless.

Laws for a Holy People (xiv–xxvi). Many of the laws given in these chapters either repeat, or expand, or modify those which are given in the preceding books. Lawful Meat (xiv. 3–21). The same general rules are to be observed as are given more fully in Leviticus xi. It is to be noted that the eating

of "game" is permitted (verse 5). The law of the *tithe* naturally follows (cf. Lev. xxvii. 30; Num. xviii. 21–32), but with
special reference to the changed conditions (xiv. 22–9).[1] The
Year of Release (xv. 1–15) expands the law already contained
in the Book of the Covenant (Exod. xxi. 2). It is an attempt
to preserve among the Israelites that equality of wealth which
has its basis in the distribution of the land by *lot,* and its
passing from generation to generation by *inheritance.* The
Bondservant for ever (verses 16–18). "For ever" means, of
course, as long as he lives. It does not include or involve the
children.

The law regarding *firstlings* and *first fruits* is followed by
instructions regarding the *three annual feasts* (xvi. 1–17).
These laws are largely a repetition of what is given in
Exodus xxiii and Leviticus xxiii. The laws laid down for
the *Judges* (verses 18–20) are brief but adequate, and as
applicable *to-day* as when first uttered. It is at times hard
to see any connection between these laws. The command
regarding the "grove" and the "idol" (xvi. 21) represents in
a sense the recurrence of that great major theme which runs
throughout the whole of Deuteronomy, separation from evil
and obedience to God. Sacrificial animals to be unblemished
(xvii. 1). This deals with a subtle temptation, which dogged
the external worship of Israel throughout the centuries. The
best commentary on it is Malachi i. 6–10. When the Christian
gives to the *Church* things that are worn out and useless, he
should remind himself of this ancient law. God does not
want our cast-offs, but our best! Idolaters to be stoned (xvii.
2–7). Again, the severity of the Law impresses us. No wonder
Josiah rent his clothes and wept, when he read of the penalties
pronounced on the breaking of the law (2 Kings xxii. 19). The
sentence of judgment (verses 8–13). The priests at the central
sanctuary are to decide all difficult questions; and their verdict is to be accepted as final, under penalty of death.

The *"priests the Levites"* (xvii. 8 f.) are mentioned here
for the first time. The "Levites" have already been referred

---

[1] Two or three tithes are prescribed in the Law: (1) the tithe given
to the Levites and shared by them with the priests (Num. xviii. 21–32;
cf. Lev. xxvii 30–33); (2) the tithe to be eaten at the central sanctuary
(Deut. xii. 5–18, xiv. 22–27); and (3) the tithe of the third year, or
"poor" tithe (Deut. xiv. 28 f., xxvi. 12–15), if it is not included in (2).

to several times (e.g. xii. 18) and in those passages the emphasis is laid on their dependent and needy condition. But here we read of a class of men whose position of authority is so great that refusal to accept their verdict is to be punished by death. This can only mean that the phrase "the priests the Levites" means Levites who are priests, i.e. the "sons of Aaron" as distinguished from the rest of the tribe of Levi. It is the claim of the critics that according to Deuteronomy every Levite was a potential priest, and that the restriction of the priesthood to the sons of Aaron was not made until post-exilic times. But this fails to do justice to the striking difference which Deuteronomy makes between the "Levites" and the "priests the Levites". The rebellion of Korah the Kohathite was a protest against this very distinction (Num. xvi. 1 f.).

The Law of the King (xvii. 14–20). That Israel was to have kings was made known already to Abraham (Gen. xvii. 16). Yet it was also to be the distinctive glory of Israel that Jehovah was her King (Exod. xv. 18, xix. 6; Deut. xxxiii. 5). This was the reason given by that crude and rugged "judge", Gideon, for refusing to accept the kingship (Judges viii. 23). How the transition from the Theocracy to the Theocratic Kingship would have been brought about if Israel had been obedient to the commands of her divine King, we cannot say. But the account of the establishing of the kingship given in 1 Samuel viii–xii is an instructive illlustration of the way in which God rules and over-rules the sinful purposes of men for the accomplishment of His holy will. The king is to "write him a copy of this law in a book" (verses 18–20; cf. Josh i. 8)—a very significant statement.

The Priests and the Levites (xviii. 1–8). The difference between "the priests the Levites" and the simple Levites appears here again quite plainly. The share of the priests in the offerings of the people was such a substantial one that they occupied a favoured position and might easily become very rich; they might easily become tyrannical (1 Sam. ii. 12–17). It may be noted that while the thirteen cities which were later assigned by Joshua (Joshua xxi) to the priests were all comparatively near to Jerusalem, the cities of the Levites were scattered all over the land, both east and west of the Jordan. This would make it likely that many Levites would be content to live within their own gates, and not come up

to the central sanctuary at all, but depend upon the tithes
to which they were entitled. This may account for the special
provision that a Levite who wished to serve at the sanctuary
was entitled, and must be permitted, to do so.

Prophecy and the Prophet (xviii. 9–22). The intense desire
of man to know the unknown future and to control it if at
all possible is strikingly indicated here. Nine ways by which
the inhabitants of Canaan sought to do this are specified and
denounced. They are not for Israel, for whom God has provided a better way of knowing His will. *"The Lord will raise
up"* a prophet. This office is a distinct vocation. It is individual
and personal, not inherited. The calls of Isaiah, of Jeremiah,
and of Ezekiel illustrate this with especial clearness and detail
(cf. also Amos vii. 14 f.). *"From the midst of thee, of thy
brethren."* Prophecy is a distinctively Israelitish phenomenon.
No other religion has anything to compare with it. Balaam
is a notable exception, but one which proves the rule! *"Like
unto me."* Moses is the great type of the supreme Prophet
who is to come (John i. 21). He must have perfect obedience
because *"I will put my words in his mouth; and he shall speak
unto them all that I shall command him"*. The true prophet
says "Thus saith the Lord". This is a prophecy which has its
complete fulfilment only in the Lord Jesus Christ, who spake
to men as never man spake (John vii. 46; Acts iii. 22 f.). But
verses 20–2 indicate quite clearly that it also refers in a very
real, though lower sense, to that great succession of prophetic
voices, whose supreme function was to point Israel to the
Prophet, Priest, and King who was to be the Saviour of Israel
and of the world. The test of true prophecy is here stated
to be its fulfilment. It must be remembered, therefore, that
this test could apply only to those "words" or "signs" which
belonged to the present or the immediate future. It seems to
be quite clear that the prophets were accredited as true
prophets by the fulfilment of their words regarding the near
future (e.g. 1 Sam. x. 1–8) and by the signs and wonders which
they performed (e.g. 1 Kings xvii. 24). Having thus been
accredited as true prophets, their predictions of the distant
future would naturally be accepted (cf. 2 Sam. vii. 12 f.), even
though this test could not in the nature of the case be applied
to them by those who heard them. It is to be noted that we
are definitely told that this important revelation was made to

Moses at Sinai nearly forty years before the moment arrived
for its disclosure to Israel. Apparently Moses withheld it until
it was needed: a sound principle of pedagogy!

The Cities of Refuge (xix. 1–13). Three cities east of the
Jordan have been assigned (iv. 41–9) and mentioned by name.
The other three (Num. xxxv. 14) are now provided for. Verses
8 f. provide further for the increase of the number of cities
from six to nine. There is no record that this increase was
ever made. It is significant that their names are not given.
This implies a date before the conquest. The *landmark*
(verse 14) determines the "inheritance" of each Israelite in
the land. To remove it is therefore a serious offence. Such
stones, bearing the emblems of the gods and with curses in-
voking their vengeance on the man who removes them, have
been found in Babylonia dating from about the time of
Joshua. *False witness* (verses 15–21) is to be punished on the
basis of justice (verse 19), not revenge (verse 21; Exod. xxi. 24;
Lev. xxiv. 20).

In *Warfare* (xx) a sharp distinction is to be made between
Canaanite cities (verses 16 f.) and those which are "very far
off" (verse 15). The principle of *corporate responsibility* is
applied in xxi. 1–9. Each town is to be held responsible for
lawlessness within its boundaries.

Family and social relations and practices of the most varied
character are dealt with in xxi. 10–xxiii. 25. They may involve
a serious moral offence, such as the breaking of the Fifth
Commandment (xxi. 18–23) and be punished by death. Or,
they may involve what seem to be trivial matters, but are
nevertheless essential to that distinctiveness which is to
characterize Israel as the people of God. To plough with an
ox and an ass (xxii. 10) was to yoke a clean and an unclean
animal together (cf. 2 Cor. vi. 14). Linen was worn by the
priests. Wool was forbidden them for the reason given in
Ezekiel xliv. 18. Hence linen and wool were not to be mixed
together. The command that the two sexes be distinguished
by their dress is especially emphasized (xxii. 5). It is "One of
the things of which we may well say with St. Paul, 'Doth
not nature itself teach you?'" The principle is a valid one;
and the extent to which it is ignored to-day is anything but
a wholesome sign. The dress of the Israelite is to be distinctive: fringes are to be worn (verse 12). Israel was to be

a peculiar people in the sense of a distinctive people. Even their clothes were to make this clear. When a Christian is afraid of being thought "peculiar" he is in danger of losing his testimony and backsliding. The reputation and rights of a virtuous wife are safeguarded (xxii. 13–19), but a guilty wife is to be stoned. Other sex crimes are briefly dealt with (verses 20–30). Chapter xxiii deals with the question as to who may or may not "enter into the congregation". It then passes on to treat of offerings and vows.

Divorce and Remarriage (xxiv. 1–4). As it stands in the Hebrew, it is uncertain whether the conditional or circumstantial clause beginning in verse 1 ends in the middle of that verse or continues to the end of verse 3. In either case the emphasis is on the inflexible rule, that if a man divorces his wife and she marries another man, she can under no circumstances return to her first husband (verse 4). He may divorce her, but let him remember that if he does so, she is dead to him for ever—clearly intended as a warning against hasty divorce!

The rest of the laws in chapters xxiv–xxvi are too varied to classify. Humane treatment of the poor is prominent among them. The widow, the orphan, the stranger, are to be helped. The law of Levirate marriage (xxv. 5–10 reminds us of Matthew xxii. 24 f. The ritual of the *First Fruits* (xxvi. 5–11) is specially interesting because it shows how concerned Moses was that the people should *remember* the past dealings of God with them and their fathers. "Syrian" is "Aramaean" in the Hebrew. It is to be noted that so-called Aramaisms in the Old Testament need not be indicative of late date, but may, in some cases at least, be archaisms, which go back even to patriarchal times.

The object of all the laws is that Israel may be indeed a "peculiar people" and a "holy people" (xxvi. 18 f.) unto the Lord their God.

BLESSINGS AND CURSES (xxvii–xxviii). The long discourse of the preceding chapters (v–xxvi) is followed by, or we may say concludes with, detailed instructions regarding that most important and memorable event (cf. xi. 29 f.) which is to take place after Israel has entered the land (Joshua viii. 30–5). The words of the Law are to be written on the plaster which

covers the great stones which form the altar. In this way
the Law as the standard of obedience of the Holy God, and
expiatory sacrifice for failure to keep the Law and transgres-
sion against it, are brought together most impressively, just as
the two Tables of the Ten Commandments were placed in
the ark which was covered by the mercy-seat. Ebal and
Gerizim, the two lofty mountains in the centre of the land,
are to be the scene of this tragically impressive ceremony—
tragic, because the curses were so much oftener merited and
visited upon Israel than the blessings. The greater emphasis
on the curses than upon the blessings (12 curses, 6 blessings)
is obviously because of the proneness of the people to disobey.
It is noteworthy that here and in Numbers v. 22 (the only
other occurrence in the Pentateuch) "amen" is the assent to
a curse (cf. Neh. v. 13). But it is also used to claim or assent
to anticipated blessings (1 Kings i. 36; Neh. viii. 6; Ps. lxxii.
19). Does Moses name these mountains rather than historic
Shechem which nestles between them, in order that every time
an Israelite catches a glimpse of them, he may be reminded
of the solemnly prophetic ceremony which took place
there?

REAFFIRMATION OF THE SINAITIC COVENANT (xxix–xxx). It is not
clear whether xxix. 1 should be regarded as marking the conclusion of the great discourse which begins at v. 1, or as introducing what immediately follows. In the Hebrew Bible it is
connected with what precedes. At any rate, we must regard
both what precedes and what follows as simply an ampli-
fication and adaptation of the Sinaitic covenant to the situation
of Israel in the land. Moses again addresses "all Israel", with
especial reference to those who had witnessed the events which
he describes.

It may be noted that "return and gather" (xxx. 3) is a
Hebrew idiom for "gather again" (Young's *Concordance*
gives twenty-nine occurrences of this rendering in the
Authorised Version). In this chapter we have a final exhortation in terms of "life and good, and death and evil" (verse
15).

FINAL INSTRUCTIONS TO THE LEADERS (xxxi). A final word of
assurance to "all Israel" (verses 1–6) is followed by a word

to Joshua (verses 7, 23), which has its echo in Joshua i. 6 f., 9, 18.

Especially significant are the definite statements which occur here (verses 9, 24, 26) and elsewhere in Deuteronomy regarding the "writing down" of the "law" in a book, and the command that the priests, or the high priest (note the "thou"), shall read this law to the people once in every seven years. There may be room for doubt as to just what is meant by "this law", whether the whole Pentateuch is meant or only the Book of Deuteronomy. But the seven days of the feast of the tabernacles would have provided ample time, and a splendid opportunity for the reading of the entire record which Jews and Christians throughout the centuries have agreed in calling "the five books of Moses". So much at least is perfectly clear, that the law which Israel was to obey was a written law, and that it was given to them by Moses at the command of God.

Moses is now to die, and Joshua is to assume the leadership (xxxi. 14). The history of the past will surely repeat itself in the future. So Moses is to write a song which is to sing itself into the hearts of the people.

THE SONG (xxxii). Like the warnings and exhortations which run through the entire Book of Deuteronomy, the *song* and the *blessing* set before Israel "life and good, and death and evil" (xxx. 15). Moses' song, like the great paean of victory in Exodus xv, shows that this great leader of men was a true poet; and the casting of his prophetic words into poetic form was with a view to impressing them on the minds of the people for generations to come. The great themes of the song are: the greatness of Israel's God (esp. verse 39), the nothingness of idols (verses 16 f, 21), His goodness to Israel (verses 10–14), Israel's stubbornness and disobedience (verses 5–6, 15–21), God's anger and His future judgments (verses 35–42). Yet it closes with the words of hope: "and will be merciful unto his land and to his people". The frequent use of the word "rock" (cf. Exod. xvii. 6) is to be noted. As to this song, we are told both that Moses was commanded to write it, that he wrote it (verse 22) and that he "spake" it in the ears of the people (verses 30–44). Yet most critics assign it to a much later date.

The Blessing of the Tribes (xxxiii). It is appropriate that Moses, like the patriarchs, should bestow a parting blessing upon the "children" who have been his care for forty years (Num. xi. 11–15). There are resemblances with Genesis xlix, but also marked differences. The language is highly poetic and decidedly difficult to interpret. The failure to mention Simeon is apparently due to the fact that this tribe was to lose its tribal identity and practically disappear (Gen. xlix. 7). Simeon apparently increased its guilt in connection with the sin of Baal-peor (Num. xxv. 14); and the tribe lost heavily in numbers during the period of the wanderings. On the other hand, the fidelity of the Levites at the time of the apostasy of the golden calf (Exod. xxxii. 26–8) is made the reason for the turning of the curse of Levi into a blessing.

The brevity of the blessing on Judah is remarkable, and the words "bring him to his people" are hard to understand. They cannot refer to the healing of the Schism. For then we should expect "bring his people to him", since Judah was and remained the royal tribe and Israel's hopes centred in the house of David. A reference to the "ancestors" of the tribe in the sense of Genesis xxv. 8 would make these words refer to the possession of Hebron and Machpelah by Judah. But such a meaning seems doubtful.

The prophecy concerning Benjamin is also quite difficult. The view is widely held that the meaning is that Benjamin is to find distinction and security in the fact that the temple will be located on her southern border. This may be true. If so, at least the last two verbs must have God as their subject. Even then to speak of God as dwelling between the shoulders of Benjamin seems a rather doubtful figure to say the least.

The blessing of Joseph is about the same length here as in Genesis xlix and resembles it to a considerable extent. It closes with a reference to the great superiority of Ephraim over Manasseh.

The blessing closes with a declaration of the uniqueness of the God of Israel who is the Source and the Guarantor of every blessing to Israel. Consequently, while several of the verbs might naturally be taken as representing the conquest of the land as already taken place (cf. Authorized Version and Revised Version), it seems proper to see in them examples of what is called the "prophetic perfect", which describes future events as if they had already taken place. To the song and the blessing we must not forget to add the *prayer* of Moses (Ps. xc), which seems to gather up all that Moses has said by way of counsel and admonition for his wayward people. It seems to echo the words of the blessing, "The eternal God is thy refuge, and underneath are the everlasting arms" (xxxiii. 27).

MOSES' DEATH (xxxiv). Having served his day and his generation in the fear of God, Moses, with this prayer of steadfast faith and quiet acquiescence in all that God has in store for the people whom he so greatly loves and on behalf of whom he has suffered so much, ascends the heights of Pisgah, views the land which he may not yet enter (Matt. xvii 3) and passes to that rest which remaineth to the people of God. His enduring epitaph is expressed in the moving words with which the book closes (verses 10–12). Who wrote them we do not know. But they are a worthy tribute to that mighty "man of God" whose deeds and words form such a marvellous record as we read them in the pages of the Pentateuch.

We read in Colossians 1:16, "For by him were all things created that are in heaven, and that are in earth"; and in the miracles of Jesus, the changing of the water into wine, the healing of the centurion's servant, the raising of the widow of Nain's son, the feeding of the five and of the four thousand, and the raising of Lazarus, we learn something of the sovereign power over nature and its laws exerted by our Lord in the days of his flesh—immediate acts of divine power. Are we not justified in inferring that a somewhat similar immediacy of action may have marked the great events of the creative days? "He spake and it was *done*." (Ps. 33:9).

APPENDIX:

THE INTERVAL THEORY

I N VIEW of the popularity of the Interval Theory as a means of harmonizing the account of Creation given in Genesis with the findings of modern science, it may be well to state somewhat more fully the serious objections to this solution of the problem.

The first objection to this theory is that it throws the account of Creation almost completely out of balance. To regard the words of Genesis i. 1 as a brief statement (or heading) which is amplified in the rest of the chapter makes this entire chapter deal with the original creation. But when verse 1 is regarded as stating or announcing—it does not describe in any way—an original creation which was reduced to desolation (verse 2) and restored in six days (verses 3–31), the character of the chapter is radically changed. It becomes almost wholly an account not of the creation, but of the re-creating or repairing of that original creation. This is the most obvious objection to this interpretation. It seems highly improbable that an original creation which according to this theory brought into existence a world of wondrous beauty would be dismissed with a single sentence and so many verses be devoted to what would be in a sense merely a restoration of it. There are other serious objections:

(i) It is hard to believe that so immense a catastrophe as would be required to reduce the original earth to a condition which is described by the words "waste and void", "deep", "darkness", would be described so briefly and in such ambiguous terms. The account of the Flood covers several chapters and is told with some detail. But, according to this interpretation, a cataclysm of vastly greater magnitude is disposed of in a single brief sentence.

(ii) Since there is no mention of time in verses 1–2, the advocates of this theory feel free to assign vast intervals of time to these verses. They can assert that the original creation took place in an instant of time or that it covered thousands or millions of years. They can hold that the destruction of this original creation required a vast period of time; and by beginning the account of the restoration of this ruined world in the second sentence of verse 2, they can even discover a third timeless period in these two verses. But it should be remembered that the greater the time which is assigned to these verses, the more difficult does it become to limit the "days" of verses 3–31 to days of twenty-four hours. While if these "days" are defined as "ages" of vast and indeterminate length, one of the great arguments in favour of this theory—that it makes it possible to take the "days" of creation literally as days of twenty-four hours—ceases to apply.

(iii) If the original creation of "the heaven and the earth" (verse 1) included the sun, moon and stars, then the word "darkness" (verse 2) must be interpreted to mean, either that the light of these bodies was extinguished by the catastrophe or that it was concealed from the earth by mists and vapours which were the result of it. To hold that the heavenly bodies were not affected by the catastrophe described in verse 2, and that the "made" of verse 14 merely means "made to appear", i.e. to "reappear", reduces the creative act of the fourth day almost to insignificance. On the other hand, the rekindling of these heavenly bodies, supposing them to have been extinguished, might be almost as great a task as their original creation.

(iv) The creation of man is definitely assigned to the sixth day. It is stated three times that God created man (generic man, male and female) on that day (verse 27). According to the interval theory this would naturally be understood to mean that the original earth was not intended to be the habitation of man, but the abode of heavenly beings, of Satan; and it would be natural to infer that the catastrophe discovered in verse 2 was the result of and the punishment for the revolt of Satan and his angels. On the other hand, it might mean that, since the original earth like the restored earth was made for man, there must have been human beings living on this earth, living there thousands or millions of years before the creation of Adam. Of such a pre-Adamite theory the Bible knows nothing. On the contrary, it traces the ancestry of all mankind to Adam, makes Adam responsible for the fallen and sinful condition of all mankind, and makes their redemption the work of the Second Adam. But if the advocate of this theory adheres to the definite statement of verse 27 that man was created on the sixth day, he is involved in serious difficulty. Either he must restrict the creation of man to a single day, or he must say that "day" means "age", an unlimited period of time. If he does the one, he will have difficulty with the evolutionary anthropologist, who will naturally and quite properly demand that he be granted the same unlimited periods of time to produce man as the geologist has been given to account for his strata and fossils. He will argue quite cogently that twenty-four-hour anthropology and limitless-time geology are so incompatible as to be practically absurd. But if for the sake of the anthropologist the sixth day is made into a sixth age of vast and indeterminate length, the same view must be taken of all the days; and these six creative ages may well suffice both geologist and anthropologist without the assumption of age-long intervals in verses 1–2.

(v) The exegetical arguments in support of this theory are very weak: (a) The conjunction "and" at the beginning of verse 2 does not prevent verse 1 from being a summary of what follows. Cf., for example, Genesis xxiv. 60–1; Exodus iv. 21–8, xl. 18–33; Numbers x. 13–28; Joshua ii. 16–20; Judges xx. 36–46; 1 Kings xviii. 31–2; Nehemiah viii. 4–8, all of which enlarge upon the summary statement which immediately precedes. The connective "and" is used much more frequently in Hebrew than in English! (b) The verb rendered "was" in the phrase "was waste and void" may have the meaning "became". But the idiom for "became" in Hebrew is "was to". Consequently to take the "was" in the sense of "became" is at least a doubtful rendering. Cf. Genesis iii. 1; Exodus i. 5; 1 Kings xiv. 30, xviii. 46; Ezra viii. 31; 2 Chronicles xiii. 2, where the same "was" occurs. (c) "Waste and void" are rare words. They occur together only three times (Gen. i. 2; Isa. xxxiv. 11; Jer. iv. 23). They suggest a state of chaos, which could either be primitive or the result of a cataclysm. (d) As stated above, "made to appear, or reappear", for the "made" of verse 14 introduces a meaning which is quite foreign to the verse, the obvious meaning of which is that the heavenly bodies were brought into being on the fourth day. (e) Isaiah

xxiv. 1 and Jeremiah iv. 23 f. are prophetic and deal with the future, not the past.

(*f*) Isaiah xlv. 18 should be rendered, "He did not create it *to be* a waste, for inhabiting he formed it." The "wasteness" or "formlessness" of the original substance out of which God formed the earth, was simply the beginning, not the goal, of creation. The chaos was to become a cosmos, a suitable place for man to dwell in.

(*g*) Isaiah xiv. 12–23 is a prophecy concerning Babylon. Ezekiel xxviii. 1–19 concerns the prince or king of Tyre. The sin with which each is charged is an arrogant pride amounting to self-deification. In both cases the language is figurative and the sin of each is the sin of Satan. Babylon is described as the "day star" (i.e. "shining one", Authorized Version, "Lucifer"), because she has said "I will ascend unto heaven". But Babylon will be cast down to hell. Tyre, likewise, is described as an "anointed cherub" in the garden of Eden, which is the garden of God. And Tyre shall be reduced to "ashes upon the earth". In each case the arrogant claim is matched only by the greatness of the fall and the wretchedness of the final state. It is the story of the Tower of Babel retold in different forms. But great caution should be exercised in applying such figurative descriptions to the explanation of Genesis i–ii. Thus, it has been suggested that the description of the garden in Ezekiel xxviii. 13 refers to an "azoic" age of the earth, because the reference is almost exclusively to minerals. Were this suggestion adopted it would contradict Genesis ii. 9 which describes the garden in terms of vegetation. When the attempt is made to treat poetic and figurative language as matter-of-fact prose, the result is often very wide of the mark, if not positively grotesque.

(*h*) The same principle applies to Job xxxviii. 7. The statement that "the morning stars sang together" must mean either that the morning stars are personified or that they represent persons. The latter interpretation is favoured by the parallel clause, "and all the sons of God shouted for joy". Since the term "sons of God" is used of the angels in Job i–ii, it is natural to infer that the angels are referred to in both parts of this verse. Genesis i says nothing about the angels. The most, then, that we can infer from this verse is that they were created before the hexameron.

This wonderful chapter has long been a storm-centre, especially so since modern science began to prove the immensity of the universe; and many scientists have not hesitated to affirm that its statements are utterly irreconcilable with the established facts of science. It is true that there is a vast difference between this account and the statements which are found in the ordinary scientific textbook. In this account God is the sole Actor and all things come into existence by virtue of His almighty fiat. Processes as secondary causes are largely if not wholly ignored. In the account given by science second causes or processes constitute the entire subject-matter of study and they are studied as purely natural processes, supernatural acts and agencies being rigidly excluded. In this respect there is an irreconcilable conflict between Genesis i and science so-called. For the one treats as supremely important what the other tends rigidly to exclude. Between a God-ignoring science and Genesis i the conflict is irreconcilable. And all who believe the Bible to be the Word of God will feel obliged to insist that a science which wishes to be called Christian strives to do full justice to the impressive and all-important emphases in the Genesis account.

There are two great temptations for the Bible-believing Christian to avoid in dealing with such a problem. On the one hand he must avoid an attitude of hostility to science or a tendency to ignore or minimize the importance of its discoveries. When Kepler said that in studying the heavens he was "thinking God's thoughts after Him", he was simply echoing David's words in Psalms viii and xix. And if the heavens which Kepler viewed through his telescope were far vaster than those which David saw with his naked eye, how vastly great should be the conception of God which is given to us by the amazing discoveries of recent years! The Bible-believer does not have to be, he cannot afford to be, an obscurantist. He may and should welcome and glory in every new and true discovery of science as a revelation of the Creator-God of whom the Bible speaks so constantly. But he should also be careful to distinguish between ascertained facts and the theories which are put forward to account for these facts. He may accept the one and feel obliged to reject the other.

The second temptation is to try to force an agreement

between the Bible and science by "wresting" the simple statements of the Bible. Since the account in Genesis i comes down to us from what might be called a pre-scientific age, it is natural to attempt to make it speak the language of modern science; and there is a danger that this will be done "by imposing upon the words of Genesis meanings which it is simply impossible that they could ever have been intended to convey". Thus, the obvious meaning of Genesis i. 14–19 would seem to be that the "greater luminaries" and the "stars" were "made" after the earth was in existence. This conflicts with the now popular Tidal Theory of the astronomers according to which the earth is an off-shoot from the sun. To meet this difficulty by assigning to the word "made" the meaning "made to appear", "made to reappear", "rekindled", with a view to making the sun older than the earth, exposes the harmonizer to the jibe uttered by Huxley many years ago: "If we are to listen to many expositors of no mean authority, we must believe that what seems so clearly defined in Genesis—as if very great pains had been taken that there should be no possibility of mistake—is not the meaning of the text at all. . . . A person who is not a Hebrew scholar can only stand aside and admire the marvellous flexibility of a language which admits of such diverse interpretations." Science may throw much light on the Bible. It may help us to understand some of its difficult passages. But to allow science to become the interpreter of the Bible and to force upon it meanings which it clearly does not and cannot have is to undermine its supreme authority as the Word of God.

It must be remembered that the Tidal Theory is a theory, not a proved fact. Let us glance at it for a moment. Because of the vastness of interstellar space, it is held that only once in about 3,000 million years would a star pass sufficiently close to the sun to draw out from it a "filament" of matter out of which the earth and the other solar planets could be evolved. It is held further that the process of evolving the earth from a segment of this gaseous filament into a habitation for man required some 4,000 million years, a total of some seven billion years! This stupendous claim brings with it others even more inconceivable. For if, as we are told, the sun has been shining at substantially the same rate as at present during the vast period of geologic time, the question naturally suggests itself, How old is the sun? And if the solar system is only one of the youngest and least significant elements which make up the Milky Way, how old must the heavens be, which contain this Galactic System and other systems vastly more remote? The answer can only be, "countless millions of years", with the emphasis on the word *countless*. In other words, time becomes practically infinite; and the Creator God of Genesis i is allowed to retire or made to retire behind infinitely long successions of time and time-consuming process. Consequently we need to remember that "One of the commonest errors is to regard time as an agent. But in reality time does nothing and is nothing. We use it as a compendious expression for all those causes which operate slowly and imperceptibly: but, unless some positive cause is in action, no change takes place in the lapse of a thousand years" (Bishop Copleston).

We may well hesitate to assert that the days of Genesis i must be taken literally as days of twenty-four hours. But we should not hesitate to assert that infinite time and endless process are no adequate substitute for or explanation of that fiat creation by an omnipotent God of which this sublime chapter speaks so clearly and emphatically. It is equally true that "one day is with the Lord as a thousand years" and that "a thousand years *are* as one day". The great word in this account of creation is "God"; and in Him we have the only key to all its mysteries and profundities.

We read in Colossians 1:16, "For by him were all things created that are in heaven, and that are in earth"; and in the miracles of Jesus, the changing of the water into wine, the healing of the centurion's servant, the raising of the widow of Nain's son, the feeding of the five and of the four thousand, and the raising of Lazarus, we learn something of the sovereign power over nature and its laws exerted by our Lord in the days of his flesh—immediate acts of divine power. Are we not justified in inferring that a somewhat similar immediacy of action may have marked the great events of the creative days? "He spake and it was *done*." (Ps. 33:9).